Roses &
HONEYSUCKLE

Finding God in the Midst of
an Ordinary Life

Roses &

HONEYSUCKLE

BONICA BROWN

Ambassador International
GREENVILLE, SOUTH CAROLINA & BELFAST, NORTHERN IRELAND
www.ambassador-international.com

Roses & Honeysuckle

Finding God in the Midst of an Ordinary Life

ISBN: 978-1-64960-626-6, paperback
eISBN: 978-1-64960-675-4

Edited by Katie Cruice Smith
Cover Design and Interior Typesetting by Karen Slayne
Ebook Conversion by Anna Riebe Raats

Ambassador International titles may be purchased in bulk for education, business, fundraising, or sales promotional use. For information, please email sales@emeraldhouse.com.

AMBASSADOR INTERNATIONAL
Emerald House
411 University Ridge, Suite B14
Greenville, SC 29601
United States
www.ambassador-international.com

AMBASSADOR BOOKS
The Mount
2 Woodstock Link
Belfast, BT6 8DD
Northern Ireland, United Kingdom
www.ambassadormedia.co.uk

The colophon is a trademark of Ambassador, a Christian publishing company.

For my sweetheart:

Thank you for all your encouragement, thought-collecting, proofreading, and shoulder to cry on. You have been my partner and my constant companion. Thank you for your love of God and your desire to build His kingdom. All my love.

For my darling ones, Joshua, Ember, Asher, and Maisie:

I wish I could be a perfect mother. Forgive my everyday failings and know that you are created in the image of God, and He doesn't create mistakes. I hope that this book is a testimony to you that your mother loved God, and my deepest desire is that you have a relationship with the Lover of your soul. I pray that you will know God intimately and lean on Him in times of trouble.

For my friend Stevy:

Thank you for your passionate zeal for God. You push me and challenge me to pursue Him in a deep and meaningful way.

Contents

Author's Note

This book has been a way of healing for me this year. It has been a chance to discover who I am, what I believe, and what I need to work on. It is written about my day-to-day life and the struggles, temptations, life-changes, hormones, sins, and joys that make me human. It is not written from the perspective of having it all together but, instead, from the mindset that I do not. I want to look to God for the answers.

While it may not apply directly to your life and circumstances, I hope it encourages you that somewhere along the way, we have something in common. We can get through the difficult things together, if by nothing else but just knowing that someone out there is going through the same thing.

I want to encourage you that "God will meet all your needs" (Phil. 4:19). He is the One Who has the answers. God is the One to look for and to ask for guidance. He loves you, sees you, and knows you intimately. And He is willing to give us above and beyond what "we ask or imagine" (Eph. 3:20). If I continued writing and was not set on finishing this book, I could write about every season of my life and how God holds me together through it all because that is what I expect of our loving and compassionate God.

Fellow tree,
Grow strong. Hold tight to God and root yourself in Him. Blossom
and bear good fruit. Pray for the other trees struggling to make it
through the vines and the seasons. Know that He is not finished with
you. If you are going through a season, then the earth remains, and
God is still in control. With much love in Christ, I pray that you grow.

Introduction

But seek first his kingdom and his righteousness, and all these things will be given to you as well. Therefore do not worry about tomorrow, for tomorrow will worry about itself. Each day has enough trouble of its own.

Matthew 6:33-34

I am typing this on a busy Sunday morning. It is time to get everyone ready for church and pack up supplies for my eight-year-old daughter's birthday party at 2:00 p.m., and suddenly, I feel the need to write a book. I am not a writer, but I feel like God is nudging me to share my story.

This week, I find myself drowning in a sea of laundry. Last week, I discovered lice on the girls' heads, which spiraled into a frenzy of washing hair and bedding and packing stuffed animals into bags. Then we got hit with a stomach bug. All the while, my husband, a teacher, is finishing up his last two weeks of school as a sponsor for the senior class. He has not been available for the everyday mess of a ship that I have been trying to keep afloat and running smoothly. Oh, and did I mention that I homeschool my kids? But in the messy whirlwind of this thing called "life," I have forgotten one thing: to seek God's face.

I was encouraged by my friend Stevy to get outside, away from the kids, and soak in some God time. I tried it that day and just felt defeated. I walked outdoors and did not know where to start. After feeling disappointed with myself for not knowing how to find God and realizing how disconnected I felt from Him, I decided to try again the next day.

So, on Friday, I awoke, determined that I needed to find God in the middle of an ordinary life that sometimes is not so ordinary. I picked up my Bible, a book I had planned on starting, and a journal. I was ready to start this thing full throttle. Surely, I would find God's face in this impromptu, one-day decision. I am not sure what I expected, but what I found was beautiful; and it was entirely God's creation and a gift. I will not say I had a supernatural face-to-face with God; but as I walked out to the smell of roses and honeysuckle, fresh and fragrant after the spring rain, I breathed in the rich aroma and thanked God for His faithfulness. I found a bench and wrote down a few thoughts before my talkative three-year-old discovered me.

The end.

Not really, but it was the end of my trying to find God that morning. I think it is important to seek His face, ask for His direction, and work toward that relationship where I am walking with Him daily. But if I am being candid, I typically just try to survive the day-to-day and only find Him at my most broken, when I cannot seem to swim above the thoughts in my head, when I desperately need Him. Maybe that is why the day-to-day does get overwhelming. He knows that I only seek Him when I need Him; so He gives me a need because He longs for a relationship where I need, want, and desire Him. God romances us with roses and honeysuckle. We are His love, His bride, and His Church.

*Keep falsehood and lies far from me; give me neither poverty nor
riches, but give me only my daily bread. Otherwise, I may have
too much and disown you and say, "Who is the LORD?" Or I may
become poor and steal, and so dishonor the name of my God.*

Proverbs 30:8-9

I have felt the strength of these verses in my life this year. I quit
my job of over twelve years as a graphic designer (working from home),
cut back on freelance photography, and decided to go full-time (with
the support of my husband) into a new job as a homeschool mom. All
these titles have defined me as a person; but I have been trying to learn
the art of budgeting, cooking, teaching, and becoming something that
does not fit a title. Keep me from poverty and keep me from riches;
give me just what I need, Lord. What a hard but necessary prayer.

Trusting God for just enough is so hard. But it is also so amazing
watching Him meet my needs. As Paul says in Philippians 4:11-13, "I am
not saying this because I am in need, for I have learned to be content
whatever the circumstances. I know what it is to be in need, and I know
what it is to have plenty. I have learned the secret of being content in
any and every situation, whether well fed or hungry, whether living in
plenty or in want. I can do all this through him who gives me strength."

You would think that seeing God's blessings—always being faithful,
always providing—I must have it all together. I mean, if you have a
God Who pursues you with roses and honeysuckle, then you must
be walking like Enoch or Moses—someone who sees God. Or maybe
when you see God's blessings again and again, miracle after miracle,
answered prayer after answered prayer, needs met, rivers split, and
manna in the desert, you become like the children of Israel, forgetting
what God has done, even though He is in a pillar of fire by night and a
cloud by day. Maybe instead of walking faithfully, you begin doubting
and complaining. I think that is why we go through hardships. That is
God's way of reminding us that He and He alone can get us through
the murk.

I am nothing special. I excel in some areas and possess certain skills and talents. However, there is always someone prettier, smarter, more talented, or more artistic than I. If you heard me singing songs of praise on a Sunday morning, you would think that this woman really takes making a "joyful *noise*" to the extreme. All that to say, I am not a rockstar, superstar, or a supermodel. I am just an ordinary mom who sings a bit too loudly and off-key, with a heart full of Jesus.

Walk this journey with me. I don't know where you are in your life. I don't know what hardships you are facing. But my prayer and hope are that if you are reading this, you are an ordinary human trying to seek God, trying to find peace and joy in the middle of the overwhelming moments of life. Let's start down this path together.

Chapter 1

Thankfulness

Give thanks in all circumstances;
for this is God's will for you in Christ Jesus.

1 Thessalonians 5:18

If you search the Scriptures, there is verse after verse of God's provision, and we are called to be thankful. As humans, we are created and designed to worship our Creator. He is the Great I AM; and He created us to praise the One *"who was, and is, and is to come"* (Rev. 4:8). We are the clay that He molded and shaped to glorify His name.

The list of thankful Scriptures is quite lengthy. Do a quick Bible search on thankfulness, and you will find many verses reminding us of our prime directive—to borrow a term from *Star Trek*.

- "Enter his gates with thanksgiving and his courts with praise; give thanks to him and praise his name" (Psalm 100:4).
- "Always giving thanks to God the Father for everything, in the name of our Lord Jesus Christ" (Eph. 5:20).
- "Devote yourselves to prayer, being watchful and thankful." (Col. 4:2).
- "Do not be anxious about anything, but in every situation, by prayer and petition, with thanksgiving, present your requests to God" (Phil. 4:6).

So, why is it so hard to thank God for everyday things? I washed four loads of laundry today: "Thank You, God, for a washer that's running, for clean clothes, and for providing for our family." That is what I should have said. Instead, I complained in my heart, "I had to wash so many clothes today. I'm exhausted, and life is hard." It is hard to be thankful on days that seem hard. One little thing after another seems to go wrong, and God's presence feels so far away. As my aunt told me the other day, "The devil is in the details," and that is the truth. All those little details can wreck a ship and sink me to my knees.

Where are you in your walk with God? Do you seek Him daily or just when there is a need? Do you talk honestly with God as your Friend, Father, and Beloved; or do you view Him as a Holy God Who seems too hard to reach? God seems to be all those titles and so much more. He is still my Father, even though I am lost in sin, sinking so deep that I cannot breathe. My Heavenly Father gently holds me in my broken days and reminds me of my worth. He is my Friend when I am alone in the car and need Someone to listen to me vent. He is my Beloved when I am so angry, ugly, and unlovable that only He can romance me back into the woman He created me to be.

The prophet Ezekiel realized this truth for himself when God told him, "I will give you a new heart and put a new spirit in you; I will remove from you your heart of stone and give you a heart of flesh" (Ezek. 36:26). Just like Ezekiel, I needed a new heart, too. My heart was so hardened with grief that it made life heavy and weighed me down. I even allowed that weight to transfer to those I loved. I do not want to feel that kind of grief again.

My mom passed away right at the beginning of the year 2020—the year that Covid reared its ugly head, and the world and churches shut down. The cancer was sudden. She was healthy and happy, but then she got sick and quickly got worse. She was not a fan of going to the doctor; and finally, when she was almost at death's door, we convinced her to go to the hospital. That was the week we found out she had cancer, the week she left us.

But I was not angry at God. I was not mad at people or life. Honestly, I was numb. I was thankful that she did not have to suffer for years, that I got to spend her last few days at her side, and that God was in every little detail of it. I understood that God knew what He was doing, but I was doing such an excellent job of accepting the loss that I did not realize that I had really buried the pain. Suddenly, I felt so alone.

I went to church the day after she passed, thinking I would be okay, and immediately regretted that decision. I suddenly felt all the stares as people looked at me and thought about how they would come to tell me how sorry they were after church. I did not want to hear their words of "comfort." I did not want sympathy. I did not want to be touched, and I did not want to end up sobbing on the middle of the floor. I just wanted my momma.

I walked out quickly and hid in the car's back seat until my husband and kids could catch up with me and get me home. Fast forward through that year, I was just surviving, watching my kids grow up without their grandma, having to explain death and grief to my almost two-year-old and why Mommy was crying again—all while trying to make the best of a complete life change. It was hard. And I was hardened. Honestly, I do not remember much of that year.

Then last summer, I went as a sponsor to a church camp for the kids. I kept up with my kids playing in the hot summer sun and fought against God in my heart. I was bitter and did not even know it. I had not run from God. I had not outwardly sinned that people could see. I did not leave my husband, abuse my kids, and run away. Like a "good, little Christian," I held all that hurt and anger inside. Sure, I lashed out at my kids, became bitter toward my father, disconnected from my family, hid in my room crying tears that would not be comforted, and felt that my husband was not doing his share of life because of my unrealistic expectations. But I kept up the image of having it all together. I continued to attend church and continued my daily Scripture-reading plan, even though the words never really sank into me. I had been going through the motions.

But that hot, sweltering day in the middle of summer, God spoke to my heart after a long day at kids' camp. He had given me a verse that weekend before camp about creating a new heart of flesh and not a heart of stone. I read those words, wondered about their meaning, highlighted them on my Bible app, and promptly forgot.

On Monday, the children's minister spoke that verse as the theme for the camp that week. She talked about how grief can harden you, and I immediately crumbled. Leading up to that moment, God had been chipping away at my stony heart. But when I heard that verse again, I knew He was coming after me, and I could not run anymore. I wept and felt my bitterness shattering into a million pieces. Suddenly, I was face-to-face with God and His mercy. Suddenly, my head was clear, and I realized how far I had been from His presence and how I had not allowed my heart to feel.

Thankful. Even in the hard? Even in the loss of a mother, a child, or a friend? Thankful. Yes, God longs for us to be thankful. In thankfulness, there is healing. In gratitude, there is hope. My story is not your story. I could not even imagine what kind of loss or hurt you have endured. I have not walked in your shoes. But I hope you find a way to thank God, even for the hard things right now, even if that means writing down a few details where you can see the good in life.

These moments make up part of your story. Looking back at the good things you have written down might help you see where God has been walking you through the hurt, the dirt, and the hard stuff. I am not saying that writing down thankful things will pull you out of depression or that life will suddenly become easier. You might not notice a difference in your circumstances, but keep pressing forward. If nothing else, you will be fulfilling your calling to bring "a sacrifice of praise" (Heb. 13:15). You will be praising a God Who sees you and cares for you.

Chapter 2

Social Snares

I cry aloud to the LORD; I lift up my voice to the LORD for mercy.
I pour out before him my complaint; before him I tell my trouble.
When my spirit grows faint within me, it is you who watch over my
way. In the path where I walk people have hidden a snare for me.
Look and see, there is no one at my right hand; no one is concerned
for me. I have no refuge; no one cares for my life. I cry to you, LORD;
I say, "You are my refuge, my portion in the land of the living."
Listen to my cry, for I am in desperate need; rescue me from those
who pursue me, for they are too strong for me. Set me free from my
prison, that I may praise your name. Then the righteous will gather
about me because of your goodness to me.

Psalm 142

The psalmist is beginning to be one of my favorite authors. He addresses his struggles of sorrow, depression, loneliness, and fear; and yet, he still thanks God amid his suffering.

Do you ever feel like no one even cares for your life? You can be surrounded by loved ones, yet you feel like you do not even matter. Some days, social media can be a snare that makes this worse. You can post something meaningful to you, and not a single person likes your post; yet you see other people post about their breakfast, and they have over one hundred likes, loves, and comments. These unfair algorithms can make you think, *What about me? Don't I matter?* As the psalmist puts it, "No one is concerned for me . . . no one cares for my life" (v. 4).

You may not be like me, but I put a lot of thought into what I post on social media. If I post it, you can be sure that I have probably spell-checked it or given it to my husband to double-check for grammar issues. I am a bit of an overthinker. Unfortunately, I care about what people think to the extreme.

If you have watched *The Office*, then you'll know this quote from Michael Scott: "Do I need to be liked? Absolutely not. I like to be liked. I enjoy being liked. I have to be liked, but it's not like this compulsive need to be liked, like my need to be praised."[1] That is me in a nutshell. I am a people-pleaser to the extreme. I have a lot of empathy, so I feel other people's emotions. I care if I hurt their feelings or if I say something wrong. Mostly, I avoid posting anything other than cute pictures of my kids because real life is dirty, messy, controversial, and complicated.

I love how my aunt calls it "Fakebook." Typically, people do not like to post the hard days. They do not post pictures of themselves without their makeup on or cleaning cat poop off the couch pillow. They do not post the days when they yelled too much at their children because of their self-doubts and anger or just because they are tired. It is hard to be authentic. So, when I post anything on social media other than cute pictures, I overthink it. I notice if my post is not "liked" or "loved" by someone. It can punch me in the gut if someone confronts me or gets offended by my words. I will delete Facebook and avoid it for days.

Is this healthy? Probably not. Is it honest? Yes, I am as flawed as the rest of humanity. This desire to be accepted is one of my many shortcomings.

Where is God in social media? How can you glorify the Father, be honest, and have a healthy relationship with people with whom you come in contact and those you only see online? How can you speak for God and not be torn apart for your testimony? I know that God can use anything for His glory. He can use what is shared on social media to help someone's heart.

---

1   *The Office*, season 4, episode 1, "Fun Run," directed by Greg Daniels, written by Greg Daniels, Ricky Gervais, and Stephen Merchant, featuring Steve Carell, Rainn Wilson, and John Krasinski, aired September 27, 2007, in broadcast syndication, NBC Universal Television, 2005.

But for me, it is hard to balance the good and the bad. Honestly, I do not know how to be bold with it. I would rather hide away than deal with the lashing tongues that rip apart what I have to say with their counter-banter or downright vicious opinions. People can be mean and hateful. Even "Christians" that you think have the same walk and faith as you can surprise you with what they are willing to say or post behind computer screens. I say things I am not always proud of, too.

Taking time off and getting away from social media helps me feel more available to the people in my everyday life. I do not want to experience the sorrow of watching the people I care about argue over the various issues of life, politics, healthcare, government control, religion, or even just the silly news about celebrities. People are not afraid to voice on the internet what they would not dare bring up in your living room; they say hateful words that they would not speak to your face.

It is easy to react, be selfish, get angry, or feel hurt by words you read online. When words are written instead of spoken, it is harder to tell the intended message. Face-to-face conversations with the exact words could mean something completely different because of the facial expressions, inflections, and hand motions. When you feel upset by something, do not react and blast back on social media. Try calling, going to lunch, or getting face-to-face if it is someone you care about and want to keep in your life.

Give the benefit of the doubt if you know their character. You might be surprised to hear their viewpoint and be able to talk through your differences. Agree to disagree. We do not always have to try to change who someone is; honestly, we cannot change their hearts or minds. We can pray for them and let God be God.

If it is just someone trolling, blocking them is more manageable than allowing that hate to take root in your heart. I am not saying we always have to back down. Sometimes, we must stand up and protect ourselves if someone is bullying us, or we must back up a friend. What

I am saying is to remember to be kind, choose your words carefully, and know when to stand back.

What about when your posts get those "likes" and "loves" that make you feel so special or if your post goes viral? You might start getting attacked by strangers. Sometimes, the trolling that goes on can weigh down a person. Why should you give people on social media the ability to bring their hate or agendas straight into your living room and your heart through your phone or computer? Psalm 119:37 says, "Turn my eyes away from worthless things; preserve my life according to your word."

Social media has its merits. The things shared are not all negative. It is a platform for people to give their opinions, sermons, testimonies, and encouragement. I can connect to my family and friends who cannot be close by. I get to see updates and pictures of my cousins, nieces, and nephews, as well as long-distance friends and their kids. There is so much good that can come from social media. But there is also a lot of negativity. There is drama that reaches out and breaks down friendships and hurts relationships, just like in real life.

When the bad things social media does to your mind and heart outweigh the good, "be careful little eyes what you see." Put in some distance, set time to disconnect, and delete the apps from your phone so you can only see them from your computer. Remove any distractions that take your eyes off of who you are in God.

Chapter 3

God-pleaser

Am I now trying to win the approval of human beings, or of God?
Or am I trying to please people? If I were still trying to please people,
I would not be a servant of Christ.

Galatians 1:10

We do not have to live our lives to please other people. I know I have already mentioned that I am a people-pleaser. I will do everything in my power to make people happy and, thus, make myself feel good. I feel accomplished and proud when I have outdone myself to make someone feel loved. But if I am honest, the outcome usually has very few rewards. I end up working hard and do not always get the praise or glory I expect. And that is the problem with being a people-pleaser.

We are designed to be God-pleasers—created to give Him credit and recognition that we might desire for ourselves. And when our heart is not in helping people for His glory, we might end up in a downward spiral of self-pity when we do not get the thanks we expect. In fact, the apostle Paul urges, "Whatever you do, work at it with all your heart, as working for the Lord, not for human masters, since you know that you will receive an inheritance from the Lord as a reward. It is the Lord Christ you are serving" (Col. 3:23-24).

When I was a kid, we did not own a dishwasher, so we kids had to wash dishes together. My older brother, Oran, told me that if you are going to do a job, you should do it right the first time. I know that is a common saying; but as a ten-year-old, I thought it was such a revolutionary concept. I have always thought that was good advice, which I have tried to remember throughout life. If you do something half-heartedly, you will usually have to do it over again or waste more time fixing your mistakes than if you had just been all-in from the beginning.

This advice holds true in more than just work-related activities; it is also true in marriage, child-raising, chores, or friendships. Be all in. Be a God-pleaser.

Sometimes, that means telling the truth, even when it hurts. Sometimes, that means getting out of bed and taking care of your kids, even when you do not feel good. Sometimes, it means sticking with training your kids to do chores, even when it is easier (and faster) to do the work yourself. I can tell you from experience that I have let my kids watch too much TV the last few years because I needed a babysitter during work hours, and it was easy to put on some cartoons or hand them my phone for a game.

But now that I am not working and they are getting older, it has been a hard transition to switch to less screen time and more reading, outdoors, and family time. If I had done things right initially, it might not be hard to limit electronics over the summer. Mothering, teaching your kids, washing dishes, and doing laundry are hard. Who am I kidding? Life is hard. But they are also all good things. There is so much good to be had from the hard stuff. I am looking forward to a challenging but worthwhile life.

We read in Romans 12:2, "Do not conform to the pattern of this world, but be transformed by the renewing of your mind. Then you will be able to test and approve what God's will is—his good, pleasing and perfect will."

God calls us to be children of the light. The Scripture says to try to discern what is pleasing to God. Sometimes, it is not all black and white. But our lives show good fruit when we do His works, love Him, seek Him earnestly, love others, be thankful, and strive toward righteousness. It is then that we are God-pleasers.

"For you were once darkness, but now you are light in the Lord. Live as children of light (for the fruit of the light consists in all goodness, righteousness and truth) and find out what pleases the Lord. Have nothing to do with the fruitless deeds of darkness, but rather expose them" (Eph. 5:8-11).

I was talking to a friend about this part of the book. She said there are days when doing the right thing feels impossible. What should you do about the days when you are depressed or in pain and even getting out of bed is a struggle? Are you held accountable on the days when you cannot function?

I am not saying that you cannot please God if you do not get it right the first time. I am saying do the best with what you have. You may not be able to reach the standard others have for you, and you might not reach the standards you have for yourself. Sometimes, we are our hardest critics. Hello, mom guilt! We are not always going to get it right, and that is where grace comes in. Yes, you should aim high, but when you miss, you move on.

Life is full of trouble. Being a Christian does not mean you have it all together. Honestly, if you want to please God, you will depend on Him to have it all together for you. You must believe that He will provide and come through when you fall short. With Him, nothing is impossible (Luke 1:37).

The writer of Hebrews tells us, "And without faith it is impossible to please God, because anyone who comes to him must believe that he exists and that he rewards those who earnestly seek him." When we worry about not meeting standards set before us by ourselves or others, it sometimes can be discouraging. Keep in mind that you have to do life your way. You must discern what pleases God and what He wants for your life and your family.

It is good to build up each other; it is good to bounce ideas off of others, to seek wisdom, and to assemble with other believers in communion. But do not start comparing talents and gifts. We are all part of the Body of Christ, and God is our Head. "The eye cannot say to the hand, 'I don't need you'" (1 Cor. 12:21). Can the pastor say to the janitor, "You're below me"? As a homeschooling mom, can I say to a mom who sends her kids to public school, "You aren't doing it right"? I do not think so. We all have abilities, and just because I am doing what I feel is best for my family does not mean it will be the best for your children or your family.

Let me be a little raw here: I admire many incredible women. Some are in a homeschool co-op with me; some are from my church; some are friends from high school and college I keep in touch with; and some are my family. All these women are talented; some are wealthy; some are zealous, on fire for God; some suffer from depression and regrets; some are moms; and some are furbaby moms. I often feel like I do not measure up to their standards.

Maybe I am not in the same tax bracket, have the same upbringing, or face the same struggles. They each bring different gifts to the table, and it is easy to get caught up in the comparison game and forget the gifts and talents I also bring. I forget that God created me fearfully and wonderfully (Psalm 139:14). He would have sent His Son to die for me alone. After all, I am His favorite (as are *all* believers), and He knows my name (Isa. 43:1). When I start worrying about not meeting their standards, I forget that I am created perfectly by God to be who I am.

The apostle Paul asks, "Am I now trying to win the approval of human beings, or of God? Or am I trying to please people? If I were still trying to please people, I would not be a servant of Christ" (Gal. 1:10).

Remember what I said before about how there is always someone better than you? Everyone's daily walk is not going to be the same. You are not going to have the same life experiences; you are not going to have the same political or religious views. I mean, take an honest look at how many different denominations of Christianity there are. If everyone saw things the same way, we would not have so many different interpretations of Scripture.

You are going to disagree with others. You will have to stand on your beliefs before God on the day of accountability. He will know who you are, what you believe, and what you have done. He knows your heart, your life, and your circumstances. As 2 Corinthians 5:10 tells us, "For we must all appear before the judgment seat of Christ, so that each of us may receive what is due us for the things done while in the body, whether good or bad."

Chapter 4

Faithful in the Waiting

He has shown you, O mortal, what is good. And what does the LORD require of you? To act justly and to love mercy and to walk humbly with your God.

Micah 6:8

While the verse seems simple enough, all the things the Lord requires of us are impossible if God is not at the center of our lives. He wants us to act justly, treat others fairly, and make impartial decisions in our personal lives and in business. As a stay-at-home and work-from-home mom, I strongly struggled with acting justly while trying to homeschool my children. I wanted to be faithful at both work and home. It is hard to be all the things for everyone and mentally and physically exhausting. I was constantly feeling like I was acting unfairly to either my boss (my aunt) because I was taking care of the kids during work time or feeling like a failure to my children by working. After all, I was either yelling at them to be quiet so Mommy could work or hiding out in the bathroom with my computer so I could lock my door and be in a Zoom meeting. Please do not get me wrong; I am very thankful God blessed me with the ability to work from home and homeschool my kids for many years.

However, the most important job I think God has given me right now is being a mom. I tried working faithfully for my aunt while raising children, but there came a point where it was too much to try to juggle both. There has to be a balance in life. Trying to maintain that balance made it hard to prioritize my children. According to Matthew 6:24, "No one can serve two masters. Either you will hate the one and love the other, or you will be devoted to the one and despise the other. You cannot serve both God and money."

I had prayed over my job for the last several years. I had been wanting to quit but had so many reasons not to. I did not want to hurt my aunt by leaving her, and I also did not want to be the one making a decision that would plummet our household finances. Trusting that only my husband's teacher income could support our family was scary. The money I earned was the fun money—eating out, date nights, vacation funds, house repairs, etc. Both my mom and my friend Stevy had been encouraging me to quit for years and to trust God to provide, so I prayed that God would impress it on my husband's heart when it was time for me to quit. It was a long wait; but this summer, God spoke, and my husband listened. He told me that he felt God had weighed it on his heart that I should not do both anymore, and it was time for me to quit.

The following Monday, I prayed and then called my aunt to have that hard talk. Or, at least, I *thought* it would be a difficult conversation, but it ended up being easy. I found out that she had been giving me different projects to try and fulfill the hours she had promised me years ago when I had started working for her; but business had been rocky, and it was getting more difficult to find things for me to do. I promised to continue working through the end of the year as needed. On the same day, God provided extra income we did not expect. He just answered a prayer, waited for us to have the faith to follow through, and then showed up with more than enough to provide for us. He is a remarkable and faithful God. And as a result, I have become much more available to my family. My mental health has improved; and I have not been as mentally, emotionally, and physically exhausted.

God does not require a lot out of His people. He wants our hearts. God wants us to live righteously but seek Him. He created humans and knows our flaws, faults, and failures. God sent His Son to die for those imperfections that separate us from Him. He knows when we cannot do everything that life demands of us, and He does not expect us to try and do it all on our own.

God's burden is light. He tells us, "'Take my yoke upon you and learn from me, for I am gentle and humble in heart, and you will find rest for your souls. For my yoke is easy and my burden is light'" (Matt. 11:29-30). We can do all things through Him (Phil. 4:13). He is our Strength, Shield, Rest, and Breath of Life. When we try to do everything on our own, that is when things go wrong. He may not have shown up when I expected and felt like my situation would never change; but when He did change things, it was the perfect timing, and everything fell into place.

I want to encourage you to trust God with whatever your struggle is. He will show up in places, times, and ways you do not expect. I know that sounds cliché, but maybe that is because it is true.

There is a song that I love right now by Elevation Worship called "Do It Again." It speaks of God's faithfulness and promises to His people. I tend to wrap myself in a protective shell of low expectations because I am afraid to expect a good outcome in life. I am so scared of disappointment, so I prefer to think of things in an "I'll pray about it, but I won't expect anything" sort of way. That way, if God fails me, it will not hurt as badly. But the crazy thing is God will never fail me.

He does not need the bumpers that I have placed in every situation because of my struggle with trust issues. You could say my faith is weak, and I do not have that mustard-seed, moving-mountains kind of faith. But what is remarkable is that God is faithful, even when we are not. Even though I may still be walking around the walls of Jerichos in my life, eventually those will fall and crumble because God said He would do it. He cannot disown Himself, and He is faithful to

His promises. "If we are faithless, he remains faithful, for he cannot disown himself" (2 Tim. 2:13).

The waiting period has taught me perseverance that I may need when we face the teen years with our children. But now that the waiting period is over, I have seen God show up for us and provide in more ways than I can count. I am able to be more present in my children's lives. I can go on field trips; join the co-ops; and sign them up for dance, basketball, tumbling, etc. I am able to actively be a part of their learning and growth. The TV is not babysitting my children full-time while I try to meet deadlines for work. I have more free time to spend with my children.

All the extra stuff we get to be involved in is great, but on the flip side of that, I can also stop doing things. If life starts to feel overwhelming and busy, I can cancel all my plans. I do not have to do the extra activities because they are not required. I can just decide that we need a day at home, read books to them, talk about God, and relish the good things the Lord has done for me. My children are becoming amazing people. I have missed out on seeing their personalities develop and watching them grow over the years because of misplaced priorities, but I finally feel like I can watch them bloom. I still need to work on my attitude some days, but I no longer feel like work is my priority.

Through this process, I am learning alongside my children. I am learning to be more dependent on God and less on my abilities. I have learned that I have limits, and pushing myself past my limits to be a supermom hurts me and those around me. I now know that our minds are truly a battlefield, and we need rest. And finally, I am learning to move past the guilt of not being able to achieve everything that society demands of women. I am learning to rely on Christ alone—He is my Strength and my Source.

Chapter 5

Stretching New Muscles

Keep your lives free from the love of money and be content with what you have, because God has said, "Never will I leave you; never will I forsake you."

Hebrews 13:5

I have been talking a lot about God's faithfulness and how He has provided for our needs as we have transitioned to one income. But I am not going to lie and say it is *all* roses (and honeysuckle). Budgeting is no joke. Our lifestyle change has been a difficult transition. I know it is worth the extra effort, but learning to do things differently is always a little daunting. The new muscles I am talking about stretching are not physical (although I need to do some stretching there, too.) Trying to budget, meal-plan, and make sure we have gas money can be discouraging. It can even make me feel guilty for buying things for myself or spending more at the grocery store than planned.

Is it a sin to mismanage your finances? This question on finances was brought up to me the other day by a friend. She did not ask the question so I could give a black-and-white answer, but rather, it was rhetorical, nudging me to pursue a deeper understanding of God's love and grace.

Scriptures are full of financial wisdom, especially if you are looking at Proverbs. The rich rule over the poor; do not be a borrower; no money equals no friends; bribes will get you far with a king, etc. In fact, it seems like most early Hebrew cultures had a bit of an obsession with money and possessions. But Jesus came and changed that view.

While it is true that God wants to bless His people beyond our requests, He does not want us to let money become our goal or our god. God wants us to give willingly, with a good heart, to those in need. He wants us to be faithful with what He gives us. He does not expect us to have it all together.

Was it Peter who could not pay the taxes, and Jesus showed him that God could provide for his need through a coin in a fish's mouth? This story is a testimony of His ability to provide for our needs daily, sometimes in ways we find silly.

"The Lord works in mysterious ways." While not found in Scripture, this is a common saying because there are times when we are just so surprised at how He shows up and provides. In fact, we read in I Corinthians 1:27, "But God chose the foolish things of the world to shame the wise; God chose the weak things of the world to shame the strong."

My husband and I are so thankful for our parents. Both of us had Christian parents who raised us in church. Not everyone has parents involved, much less active, in a church. We do not discount how blessed we are to have the background that we have. Because of how they have influenced our lives, we have a great marriage. My parents have been an enormous help in our early years of marriage because they were available most weekends to be our babysitters. We became involved as youth pastors in our church because of their willingness to watch our kids so we could help plan things and be at the events. We even had date weekends. It was a blessing to get an entire night of sleep on a Friday while our four young kids visited their grandparents.

That season of life changed, as life always has a way of doing. When my mom passed away, we were suddenly on our own. My dad is usually busy working and is not able to be a babysitter. My husband's parents are great; but with ten grandkids under the age of ten, they do not have the time to babysit our kids very often. Life flipped from lots of help with our children to suddenly swimming in quality family time with our kids.

As I said before, my current God-given role is being a mom. I do not want to blink or wish away these precious years with my children. I am just being honest that it is challenging to be constantly around my kids without a break. Peace, quiet, alone time, and time with you and your spouse revitalize a marriage. The need for quiet time is especially true when you have a talkative three-year-old who seems to have almost a college-age vocabulary.

Since date nights are rare and there is an added need to stay on a new budget, we are stretching those muscles to figure out fun and affordable things to do. The other day, my husband and I walked around the park on a date for the first time in years. It was beautiful outside and felt fresh and romantic. It was an encouraging reminder our marriage does not need an expensive day of shopping or a weekend getaway to survive—not that those things are wrong or entirely out of the question, but not making it a regular habit makes our getaway days more special. This summer, we are also starting a new system to take turns with the kids to let each other get some quiet time to go on a drive or eat alone. We hope this gift of time for each other will give both of us rest and time for renewal in our marriage and with God. We are in a new season in this ever-changing life, but it is worth embracing.

Chapter 6

Rocks Cry Out

The heavens declare the glory of God; the skies proclaim the work of his hands. Day after day they pour forth speech; night after night they reveal knowledge. They have no speech, they use no words; no sound is heard from them. Yet their voice goes out into all the earth, their words to the ends of the world. In the heavens God has pitched a tent for the sun. It is like a bridegroom coming out of his chamber, like a champion rejoicing to run his course. It rises at one end of the heavens and makes its circuit to the other; nothing is deprived of its warmth."

Psalm 19:1-6

What does it mean to praise God? Praise means "an expression of approval."[2] Because of all God has done, we have so many reasons to praise Him. God created the heavens and the earth, life and breath, you and me. His wonderful creation is all around us in every single breath we take.

Yesterday, I lay outside on a little patch of grass in the warm summer sun and looked up. The sky was clear blue. I felt the sky was almost tangible; but when I reached up, it continued forever, a vast, infinite blue space floating above my head. How can you look at an orange sunset and not admire God? Or when you look up at the night sky, with thousands of stars *just* out of reach, how can you not see Him in His creation?

---

2   *Merriam-Webster Dictionary*, s.v. "Praise," accessed May 28, 2023, https://www.merriam-webster.com/dictionary/praise.

The sky praises God. The earth glorifies God. All of His creation praises Him. But we humans are set apart from everything else that He made. We are not stars, trees, rocks, or beasts of the earth; yet God longs for His people to praise him. He is our very Breath and Life. Marvelous are His works (Psalm 139:14).

"We are all the work of [His] hand" (Isa. 64:8). He created us. Let that sink in. God could make anything to praise His name, but He created something special. He created us to be above all of His creation and specifically designed us to glorify Him. But do we? Do we praise Him for His marvelous works? Do we praise Him for His mercy and grace? Do we praise Him for loving us and making us His favorite creation? Are we doing what we were created to do?

In Luke 19:37-40, Jesus tells the religious leaders that if He were to stop people from praising Him, the rocks would cry out because God is worth praising.

> When he came near the place where the road goes down the Mount of Olives, the whole crowd of disciples began joyfully to praise God in loud voices for all the miracles they had seen: "Blessed is the king who comes in the name of the Lord!" "Peace in heaven and glory in the highest!" Some of the Pharisees in the crowd said to Jesus, "Teacher, rebuke your disciples!" "I tell you," he replied, "if they keep quiet, the stones will cry out."

Self-sufficient. Self-reliant. Self-righteous. Selfish. People do not want to praise God because they do not like to acknowledge their need for Him. Without a God, we can do whatever we want and whatever feels good to us. We do not have to worry about being judged. The Scriptures say God is more than just a Judge. He is fair, righteous, and holy; but most importantly, He is loving and quick to forgive us. What an awesome God He is! We need Him in every aspect of our lives. But when we think we have it all together and forget to thank Him, praise Him, or even acknowledge Him, we are ultimately separated from Him. What a lonely place to be.

I started this book in that lonely place. I realized I was missing God's presence and needed to find Him. I was not lost. I was not living a life of sin—at least, not the visible kind. Even though I looked righteous, there was a separation from His presence. I was not seeking Him because I was in a comfortable place. I felt like I was good. Oh, how wrong I was! Spiritually, I was in still, shallow water and did not want to go deeper. The water was getting stagnant, contaminated, and full of disappointment. I needed the fresh Living Water to renew my heart like Jesus offered to the woman at the well in John 4: "Jesus answered her, 'If you knew the gift of God and who it is that asks you for a drink, you would have asked him and he would have given you living water.' Jesus answered, 'Everyone who drinks this water will be thirsty again, but whoever drinks the water I give them will never thirst. Indeed, the water I give them will become in them a spring of water welling up to eternal life'" (John 4:10, 13-14).

In the process of my seeking Jesus, He is drawing me nearer. He is closing the gap that I put between us. I want to praise Him, and He desires my praise. He created each of us for that very purpose. I felt inspired to seek after Him and proclaim His goodness; I wanted to be on fire for Him. But at this moment, I feel like words are hard to find. That is how it goes sometimes. God is so good, but we are just people. We fizzle and fade, getting caught up in the nitty-gritty of everyday life. We get tired.

I do not know about you, but I feel lost in this tired, lonely place. I need Jesus—His peace, rest, and restoration. I need a revival. God designed us to be vessels filled up and pouring over with His Spirit. But if we are not full vessels, we will not overflow with His love for others, and our lives will quit being fruitful and reflecting His goodness.

When we praise God, we are honoring Him. We are acknowledging our need for Him. We are saying that He is worthy. We are humbling ourselves, becoming vulnerable, and ultimately surrendering our lives to Him. And through this process of humbling ourselves, submitting to His will, and glorifying His name, He is creating a new work in us.

I have been on a journey with God learning Who He is and learning who I am in Him. Honestly, I did not have much experience with the Holy Spirit as an active part of my life. I grew up in a little Bible church, mostly comprised of our family and an older congregation. It was a sweet church community, and I loved the people there. I am so thankful for my parents raising me in church and teaching me about God. They taught biblical truth, yet I feel they missed much of Who God is. The focus was on rules and regulations and less on the relationship with God. The little "Church of the Open Door" ended up closing their door soon after I married and started attending my husband's church.

It is sad when a church dies. The congregation grows old and gets set in their ways, and the Spirit of God is not alive and active. Maybe that is how we get in our walk with God. We get set in our ways, stop watering and adding nutrients to the soil of our hearts; and eventually, we stop growing. I want so much more of God than that. I want to live a life of praise, hear God's voice, and walk and talk with Him. I want Him to be my Everything. How do we get there?

I believe there are essential seasons of growth. Perhaps I needed a more legalistic upbringing so that when I felt God's grace and mercy, I could see how wonderful He is. I could see Him as more than a great, mighty, distant God, Who would strike me down for sinning. Instead, I see Him as a Father, Friend, and Soulmate, Who knows my innermost being. Perhaps I needed a season of stillness, of being stuck, so when I felt His presence again, I would dive into the deep waters and grow.

Chapter 7

Lord, Teach Us to Pray

"Ask and it will be given to you; seek and you will find;
knock and the door will be opened to you."

Matthew 7:7

God's Word tells us to ask Him for what we want and need. He knows our needs, but He wants us to ask. Are we afraid to ask for a specific answer because we fear God does not want that for us and will tell us no? Or sometimes, it is the opposite, and we worry that He will say yes. We might get what we asked for, and it might not be what we thought. We fear the unknown and expect the worst.

But if we walk with God and trust Him, we have to have faith that He will meet our needs. Matthew 7:9-11 asks, "'Which of you, if your son asks for bread, will give him a stone? . . . If you, then, though you are evil, know how to give good gifts to your children, how much more will your Father in heaven give good gifts to those who ask him!'" If you ask for healing, will He cause you to be worse off as punishment for you approaching Him in that way? No, He cares about our wants and our needs. Through Jesus, we can go boldly before the throne of God to ask Him for the things we desire. We are no longer unclean and unholy because Jesus' blood covers our shame.

According to 1 Peter 5:6-7, "Humble yourselves, therefore, under God's mighty hand, that he may lift you up in due time. Cast all your anxiety on him because he cares for you." He wants to meet our needs. I am not doing a "name it, claim it" thing here. I know that gets a bad rap. Instead of preaching riches, I am just rhetorically asking, "Why don't we ask God for it?" Here are some examples of daily things for which I ask God's help:

- Lost keys
- A bad day
- Financial problems
- Moments of anxiety
- Stubbed toes
- Fighting kids
- Missing chickens because I forgot to lock the coop
- Forgetfulness
- Loneliness

God wants to hear about our daily struggles and anxiety. He cares. The Bible tells us in Psalm 145:18-19, "The LORD is near to all who call on him, to all who call on him in truth. He fulfills the desires of those who fear him; he hears their cry and saves them."

He wants us to trust Him so completely that we do not have to worry or fear. In this life, we will go through things, but do not let those things take over your heart. Do not let them be like vines that choke out all the life in your growth. We live in a broken world. Our choices affect others, and other people's actions affect us. We will not get it perfect. We are not promised an easy life, but we are promised that He will see us through. Do not lose faith in God. If we live with God as our focus, our wants and desires will align with His. What an amazing God He is for caring for us.

We can see a list of those things that align with God's wants and desires in 1 Thessalonians 5:14-19:

And we urge you, brothers and sisters, warn those who are idle and disruptive, encourage the disheartened, help the weak, be patient with everyone. Make sure that nobody pays back wrong for wrong, but always strive to do what is good for each other and for everyone else. Rejoice always, pray continually, give thanks in all circumstances; for this is God's will for you in Christ Jesus. Do not quench the Spirit.

I like verse seventeen: "pray continually." Obviously, you cannot pray all day long without taking time to talk to other people or to eat. But you *can* have a heart that is open to His voice every moment. We need to live in constant communication with the Father. Tell Him about what is going on with you. Tell Him your every weakness, fear, and trouble, as well as the good stuff. It is like asking your kids at the table how their day was without much of a response. You teach your kids to communicate with you, and God wants the same of us. Good relationships require good communication. Communication is essential for friendships, marriage, work, and a spiritual walk with God.

Praying continually also means we should not give up bringing our petitions to God. It is easy to think that there will never be change; the person will never come to Christ; the habit will never be broken; the attitude will never soften. "Pray continually." When you need an answer from God, keep asking in faith. Sometimes, we do not see an answer to the problem. It is easy to give up and think that change will never happen; but God can soften hearts, heal wounds, and restore His people.

Chapter 8

Black, White, and Shades of Gray

What shall we say, then? Shall we go on sinning so that grace may increase? By no means! We are those who have died to sin; how can we live in it any longer?

Romans 6:1-2

I have been talking about God's grace and mercy and how He is faithful to us even when we are not faithful to Him. But does that give us an excuse to sin? The Scriptures say no. Just because we can rest in His reassuring grace does not mean we are exempt from holding ourselves and other Christians accountable. We cannot go on sinning and not expect consequences. God calls Christians to a higher standard than the world. Unbelievers may choose to deny the facts; but ultimately, all creation knows there is a God but refuses to thank Him, honor Him, or even acknowledge Him. They are "wise in their own eyes" (Prov. 3:7).

It is easy to be lifted in pride and think you have it all together. If you are not careful, you can start to look about the same as everyone else. It is pretty easy to fit in with the world when you are not deep in your walk with God. Sometimes, we get caught up in keeping up with the Joneses; we strive for a bigger house, more stuff, a better job, etc. We want the things that make us look good and feel good. But we need to remember what God says about chasing after the things of this world:

The wrath of God is being revealed from heaven against all the godlessness and wickedness of people, who suppress the truth by their wickedness, since what may be known about God is plain to them, because God has made it plain to them. For since the creation of the world God's invisible qualities—his eternal power and divine nature—have been clearly seen, being understood from what has been made, so that people are without excuse. For although they knew God, they neither glorified him as God nor gave thanks to him, but their thinking became futile and their foolish hearts were darkened. Although they claimed to be wise, they became fools and exchanged the glory of the immortal God for images made to look like a mortal human being and birds and animals and reptiles. Therefore God gave them over in the sinful desires of their hearts to sexual impurity for the degrading of their bodies with one another. They exchanged the truth about God for a lie, and worshiped and served created things rather than the Creator—who is forever praised. Amen (Rom. 1:18-25).

So, what does it mean to be "of the world"? That phrase is used a lot in Christian communities. The Church seems to sum it up by how people look, act, and speak; what music they listen to; their lifestyle; and the sins that define them. But we should not get too caught up in outward appearances. Instead, we should define the "world" as selfishness and pride. And "Christians" can be pretty selfish, too.

I know I am stepping on toes—mine included. Just because you are looking and acting the part does not mean all is right in your heart. (I like that little rhyme there.) The world wants the things that benefit them and feel good. Is that not what we want, too?

I think we are all a little worldly when we are selfish or when we forget to have a giving heart when we look down on others because they do not match our living standards. It is easy to turn a blind eye and keep driving when someone is holding a sign at the street corner asking for help. I have done it. And instead of trusting that God will do more with our willing heart than we can imagine, we like to justify it by saying that they will just use the money for beer or cigarettes. We must trust that when we stop to help, there are witnesses to our good deeds. We are sowing good seeds for God's kingdom. And without even realizing it, we are testifying about Who God is.

Our children will ask why we are helping and learn to be kind to those in need. Being a part of this "world" is only doing those good things when we think people are looking. The Scriptures give many examples of the religious leaders in Jesus' time—you know, the ones who were the example of godliness and holiness, the ones who were supposed to be up close and personal with God—and Jesus condemned them for announcing their giving and tithing. He points out that they give and pray these elaborate prayers so everyone can see their "goodness." They were tooting their own horns. The ones supposed to have it all together—the wealthy, nicely dressed, "godly" leaders—were doing it as a show. Their exterior looked like they had it right, but inside, these leaders did not have their hearts lined up with God's.

It is easy to look at Scripture and fit it to meet our beliefs and lifestyle. Not everything written is black and white. Sometimes, things are not clearly defined as "sin" in Scripture. Because of this, you can probably justify doing things that are not good for you and even twist Scripture to back up what you believe. This type of justification is reading between the lines. Just because you can justify your actions does not mean that you are in good standing with God or that your heart is right. It also does not mean that everything you do is good for you. This reading between the lines is where the "shades of gray" come in.

Paul used the analogy of running a race as an example for living this life (1 Cor. 9:24-27). Not everything you do will disqualify you from the race; but if you add weights to your life that are not lining up with God's perfect plan, they can slow you down, making it a lot harder to cross that finish line. Your focus can get sidetracked. Sometimes, we focus our time and energy on work, chores, errands, DIY projects, hobbies, watching TV, going on vacations, etc., which can be good things. They enhance your quality of life and give you downtime or family time; some are necessities. I mean, if you do not work, you do not eat, right (2 Thess. 2:10)?

*So, in and of themselves, the things we do in life are usually es*sential and good. Here is where the "but" comes in. When you are living life and doing all the good things *but* forget to pray or take time for God during your day, these things take over your heart and become your focus and priority. Instead of inherently good things, they become weights and vines in the way of your walk and growth with God.

I am saying this for myself. I have these selfish ambitions. I want to look good and have a good name. I want to be seen by others as good. Remember, I am a people-pleaser. I do not want to be at enmity with anyone. I want to accept everyone, and I want to be accepted and loved by everyone. I want to see the good in people. Unfortunately, that is unrealistic. The Bible says that no one is perfect and that all are sinners (Rom. 3:10-12). There are dangerous people—murderers, rapists, liars, thieves, bullies, addicts, and sinners. We live in a broken world.

The difference between being a "Christian" or part of the "world" is not that Christians suddenly have it all together. We still make mistakes. We are still flesh-and-blood humans with hurts, shame, sins, and blots on our record. We are still selfish, broken individuals who fail. We still do things that separate us from God.

The difference is that God no longer sees those blots. His blood washes away the stain. He has wiped the slate clean and continues to give grace and love. The separation from God that once existed is no more. Once you have accepted Jesus, He starts working on your heart, changing you from the inside out. It might take some time. You might still look and act like the world. But as you grow, you change. Your priorities change. You start looking a little less like this world and a little more like Jesus. You morph from a caterpillar into a butterfly. You become a new creation. God wants us to look, act, and *be* different.

Chapter 9

Teaching Our Children

All Scripture is God-breathed and is useful for teaching,
rebuking, correcting and training in righteousness.

2 Timothy 3:16

God inspires everything in Scripture. God wrote His Word to fit each person's need to hear it. Some of the doctrine questions Christians argue over are for growth. Perhaps the different interpretations cause us to wrestle with what we know, look at things with fresh eyes, and then apply that knowledge in our walk with God. This struggle helps us to own our truths and apply them to our hearts. Salvation does not come through our parents' or grandparents' beliefs alone. We have to have our own faith, our own beliefs, and our own walk.

In the same perspective, we cannot save our children through our faith. We can teach them about God and trust that God will work on their hearts. But in the end, their walk with God has to be their own. As a parent, that is a hard pill to swallow, and I hope my children accept God and reach that point of maturity in their walk with Him.

I want my children to know God. I want them to walk with Him, talk with Him, and be even closer in their walk with Him than I could imagine. But I can only teach them what I know. I can tell them my testimony and His story, read the Scriptures, and train them to be "good" kids. But as they grow into teenagers and young adults, they will have to make the decisions that will ultimately lead them to God or not. I pray they will find truth in their lives.

But what is truth? Pilate asked that same question to Jesus in John 18:37-38: *"'You are a king, then!'* said Pilate. Jesus answered, 'You say that I am a king. In fact, the reason I was born and came into the world is to testify to the truth. Everyone on the side of truth listens to me.' 'What is truth?' retorted Pilate. With this he went out again to the Jews gathered there and said, 'I find no basis for a charge against him.'"

Jesus is "the way and the truth and the life" (John 14:6). His genuineness catches the world off guard because people are used to the opposite. Cheating, lies, gossip, cutting in line, bribes, dishonest gain—that is how you get ahead in life. Most people seek after truth, and Pilate was no different; but the irony is that the Truth was standing right in front of him, and he did not realize it.

As parents, our job is to teach our children the truth of Who God is. We can guide them with our words; but as they grow up, our children will be watching our actions. If our lives line up with the world instead of with the Word of God, then that is what our children will imitate. We must strive to walk closer with God—not just for ourselves, but also for our children and children's children, to a thousand generations. What a breathtaking promise! God gives to those He loves and who love Him in return. And we can have faith that if we do our best, God will meet us on the other end. He will make up for the slack.

So, what can we do in the meantime? "Let us not become weary in doing good, for at the proper time we will reap a harvest if we do not give up" (Gal. 6:9). Talking the talk is easy, but walking the walk is hard. I think that is almost the theme of this book—living for God is *hard*. It is not going to be easy to live a life for God. It is not easy to always do good, and we often get weary. We let our failures and faults hinder our walk with Him. Isaiah 40:31 says not to give up hope: "But those who hope in the LORD will renew their strength. They will soar on wings like eagles; they will run and not grow weary, they will walk and not be faint." We are just vessels that God can remake, remold, refresh, and renew.

Only through God's love, grace, and mercy can we lead our children to the truth. We will fail. In this life, we will have trouble, but God gives us hope. To renew means "to resume again."[3] What an amazing God. We may fail and quit, but that does not mean He leaves or abandons us. When we get to that point in our lives when we are weary, things are complicated, and we only see our failures, that is when He starts something new in us. He lets the interruptions happen for our benefit, and then He allows us to resume our walk with Him.

Our kids can see all our imperfections, struggles, and growth. Maybe God designed it so that as our children grow and have struggles, they will see our examples and have hope for a brighter tomorrow. After all, they can see how God worked things out for their parents and their grandparents.

---

3   *Merriam-Webster Dictionary,* s.v. "Renew," accessed May 28, 2023, https://www.merriam-webster.com/dictionary/renew.

Chapter 10

Worthwhile

For you created my inmost being; you knit me together in my mother's womb. I praise you because I am fearfully and wonderfully made; your works are wonderful, I know that full well.

Psalm 139:13-14

Sometimes, I get that entitled feeling that says, "I am being undervalued and worth so much more." Entitlement is a dangerous, disappointing, and hurtful place to be; but the opposite of that is an even more dangerous place. Something that has been weighing on me is my worth in Christ and in life. Honestly, the word *worthless* keeps popping into my head. I know, we all have worth to God. That just is not the story that I tell myself. Feeling worthless, like trash that needs to be taken out, is a lie that can pull me down into the depths of despair quickly.

So, what determines our worth as people? Are you only worthwhile if you have something to contribute to society, to God, or to others? Is it your job, title, or income that gives you a purpose or value?

Worth is defined as "the value of something measured by its qualities or by the esteem in which it is held."[4] So, what gives me value or that ten-star rating that people prize? We all want to be useful, needed, and valued. What if we are not? What If we feel like we have absolutely no value in our situations and with the people surrounding us? I am

---

4   *Merriam-Webster Dictionary,* s.v. "Worth," accessed May 28, 2023, https://www.merriam-webster.com/dictionary/worth.

speaking of the lies that we tell ourselves in those dark places when we feel like we have no purpose.

Women are twice as likely as men to experience depression and go through feelings of worthlessness. Why is that? Are we told things throughout our lives that cause us to feel like we are not measuring up?

We have the example of the virtuous woman in Proverbs 31 to use as a role model. This woman is like a gem; she is so desirable but almost impossible to find. Maybe it is because that is a lot of expectations to have for someone—either male or female. This woman knows how to weave fabric, sew clothes for her household, be a gardener, cook, act as a real estate agent, keep house, manage money, exercise, and never sleep. By getting up early and going to bed late, she shows that she is diligent, faithful, hardworking, wise, and has a heart for God. She is the one behind the scenes making a good name for her husband at the gate. She is, by definition, the perfect "Stepford wife." If I am comparing myself to her, I fall really, really short.

I know that the Scriptures tell the stories of Enoch, Abraham, Moses, Elijah, David, etc. I could go on; most of the Bible talks about men who walked closely to God. Men are made in the image of God. Women are to be submissive to their husbands, quiet, meek, and modest. There are stories of women in there, but honestly, from the time of Creation itself, women seem to come second. We are the weaker vessels, the "helpmeets" of our male counterparts.

On a personal level, I am fine with that position. I do not want to be the leader of my marriage or front-and-center in life. I want my husband to be the leader of our family and household. But I also want to feel valued. I want my opinions to matter and be considered. Do not get me wrong—my husband is great. Honestly, he treats me like I am an equal partner in our home. He loves me and values me. But that does not mean I always feel that value. I still had hurt and anger from being overlooked when I was a little girl, of coming in second place to my brothers. I spent most of my life fighting those feelings of not having value. They pushed me into wanting to be smarter, tougher, and more athletic because I wanted to compete with the attention that my brothers received. I wanted to be valued.

My father and I have had some really good, honest conversations—more so now that my mom has passed away. He does listen to my opinions, and when I was growing up, I was given a chance to state my case and defend my ideas. Sometimes, he would change his mind on a no answer because I had a good enough counter-argument to change his mind. However, if that opinion were to conflict with that of one of my brothers, their ideas would hold more weight and value than mine. I do not think he intended to make me feel second-rate to my brothers, but I did feel that on a huge scale. So, when the thought that says I am worthless rears its ugly head, I am at its disposal.

God did not create women to be worthless, but He also did not create them to be of greater value than men. God did not make a mistake when He created man. He did not say, "Whoops, let's fix this." But sometimes, as women, we think we need to "fix" our spouses. Honestly, I think when God created Adam, it would have been enough. Adam and God for all eternity. But God knew that Adam would desire more than just Him. This is the first part of the creation story where God says, "It is not good" (Gen. 2:18). God knew that Adam would sin, and he would have most likely been tempted to disobey with or without a woman, so He made "a helper suitable for him" (Gen. 2:18).

In His mercy, God knew that man would need companionship when he became separated from Him. God showed Adam grace even before he needed it! Perhaps Eve was added in after all the animals were named so that Adam had a chance to see there was no one just like him. That way, when he saw Eve for the first time, he would know her value. Once God created Eve, Adam was ecstatic; he knew what stood before him was a perfect counterpart to him. That is how men should view women—not as less than themselves, but as something to treasure, as their own body.

When God created Adam, He said what He created was good. When God created Eve, it was also good. Together we are "mankind," created in the image of God. Genesis 1:27 says, "So God created mankind in his own image, in the image of God he created them; male and female he created them." He designed both males and females for a purpose. We are not worthless. We have more value than all the rest of His creation, even above the angels.

The New Testament has a *lot* of Scriptures that can be taken as "putting your women folk in their place." And sometimes, that becomes the focus for men who want submissive wives. They use (and abuse) those Scriptures to dominate their households. But the Bible also talks about husbands loving their wives as they love their own bodies (Eph. 5:23). Do men read that and obey that verse? I think that before a husband can expect his wife to be submissive and respectful, he must first work on his own heart. If a husband truly loves his wife as his own body, as Christ intended, then a wife will long to do the things that are asked of her. If she feels treasured, she will go above and beyond to make a haven for her husband at home. She will become that Proverbs 31 woman at heart because she will know her worth and her value. What a beautiful picture of what God intended for us. But it only comes with a husband treating his spouse with love, not as an overlord.

In the same regard, if you, as a woman, want to be treated with love and respect, then you must also do your part to submit to your husband's authority. Even if he is falling a little short on keeping up his part of the Scripture, when you show that respect and submission, you will change his heart to value and love you more. Honestly, in regards to marriage, God created a perfect picture of how a relationship should work. It is when we let our hearts harden that things fall out of place and feel broken.

It is not easy to be transparent and vulnerable with your spouse. It is not always easy to love each other. We do not always agree or get along. Marriage can be hard; but when you love, respect, and value each other, it becomes a whole lot easier.

Of course, as a disclaimer, I am referencing relationships between believers, with God at the center. If you are unequally yoked with an unbeliever (2 Cor. 6:14), then you should not be submissive to things that do not line up with Scripture. Your relationship with God should always go above your relationships with other people, including your spouse.

I pray that you know you are loved, valued, and cared about. I pray that you find your worth in Christ and that you know you are a precious gem, even if you do not know how to cook, sew, or weave fine linen fabric. Christ died for you. He died for the Church and for every single believer who belongs to His family. You are not trash. You are not overlooked. You are not alone. Your worth is not defined by human standards. You do not have to have a title, money, kids, or a husband; write a book; or be a great leader. You definitely do not have to have it all together. "But God demonstrates his own love for us in this: While we were still sinners, Christ died for us" (Rom. 5:8).

He knows the very hairs on your head—every single strand of hair (Luke 12:7). (I told you I spent a lot of time combing nits out of my girls' hair this summer, so believe me that I know how impossible that would be to count.) And He would do that for each and every one of us. He is the Potter, and we are the clay (Isa. 64:8). He formed us for a purpose. We do not always see what that purpose is. Sometimes, it is so hard to trust God; it is like looking through the dark glass trying to figure out our purpose and our worth. We are dust; but like gold, we just have to be refined. We are His most valuable possession.

My parents tried their best to raise their seven kids. They did not always make the right decisions. They are human, and their actions and mistakes affected their children both positively and negatively. I have started to learn to give them grace. I want that grace with my own children when I make mistakes. I am human, and I will not get it all right. I hope that I do not hurt my children with my words or actions; but it is easy to get angry, tired, and to make mistakes.

It is easy to follow the road most traveled in life, marriage, and parenting. It is hard to give grace, forgiveness, and mercy. Honestly, through this book, I have been able to come to terms with some of the things I did not realize I was holding onto. Through writing down the past, I have been able to see more clearly the things that I was angry about—the hurt and disappointments deep in my heart.

The illusions I had of having perfect parents came crashing down; and with that crash came relief that even if I mess up with my children, I am still doing okay. Like them, I have to trust that God will come in where I fall short. I will live my life walking the hard path so that my children will "arise and call [me] blessed" and that my husband will be proud of me (Prov. 31:23, 28). I have to trust that I will become the virtuous woman who is hard to find—not because of what I can do in my own power and strength but because I have a God Who directs my steps.

Chapter 11

Fear Not

Do not be anxious about anything, but in every situation,
by prayer and petition, with thanksgiving, present your requests to
God. And the peace of God, which transcends all understanding,
will guard your hearts and your minds in Christ Jesus.

Philippians 4:6-7

"Do not be anxious about anything"? How, Lord? How do we put down the things that cause our hearts to fear? I think He gives us that answer in the second part of that verse: "with thanksgiving." God is a God of peace. He wants us to trust Him. He wants our faith.

Here is a raw piece of me. I am fearful. Little things can feel like mountains to me. One broken thing happens, and I am a broken mess on the floor. Creating and designing websites have been part of my professional life since I graduated from college. They are not what I went to college for. In fact, almost everything I know about websites has been self-taught out of necessity in my career. So, I feel like a fraud or an imposter when I am working on a website.

When something goes wrong with a website I created, my face gets hot and flushed; my heart beats ridiculously fast; and I feel like I cannot do anything but curl up into the fetal position. My brain completely shuts down. Up until recent years, I had never really experienced an anxiety attack like what I feel when it comes to coding. On the flip side of things, I am actually pretty good at websites. They break me completely. But they are also something I have learned and have a bit of a talent for. But the fear causes me to feel insufficient.

I am going to take a step here and say I am not the only one who has something like this in my life. Websites are my weakness. They terrify me, but if I was not so afraid, they could be something that God uses for His purposes. But the enemy has planted seeds of fear and doubt that I cannot seem to weed out.

Remember Moses? He was that guy from the Old Testament who led the Israelites out of slavery in Egypt. He was the one who led them across the Red Sea on dry land. He saw God pass in front of him. He was so close to God that his face was illuminated from being in His presence. He is the same guy who ran from Egypt in fear and shame, who doubted himself and God. He doubted his ability to the point he asked God to send someone else. He told God that he was not qualified; he could not speak well. He doubted himself. Yet God still used him. God still had a purpose for him. He was not qualified in his own eyes, but God qualified him.

I am not saying I am going to suddenly overcome my fears. What I am saying is even though I do not feel qualified for so many things in this life, God still has a purpose for me. I am not qualified in my eyes, but through God, I am more than enough. And so are you. He can use me. The example of my website-creating ability was just to show you how a spirit of fear can grow and how the enemy can use it to win some battles. But that fear is not from God. As 2 Timothy 1:7 reminds us, "For the Spirit God gave us does not make us timid, but gives us power, love and self-discipline."

Recently, I had to take an intruder safety training class with my homeschool group. The speaker was really qualified and had some great information. However, I left the training feeling so fearful. I agreed with the guy that it is important to be prepared. It is important to protect the lives of your children, yourself, your loved ones, and your neighbor. But holding onto fear to the point where you walk into a store with your family and feel like everyone is out to harm you is not really living a life of freedom and reliance on God. As Christians, we are called to help the helpless, to turn the other cheek, to give cheerfully out of our abundance, and to entertain angels in disguise. If we were to really live the life Christ modeled, our churches would look a whole lot different. If I were to really live as Christ modeled, I would look a whole lot different, too.

Imagine living boldly for God, not holding on to fear but resting in His power, His love, and His soundness of mind. Sometimes, the simplest of concepts like" do not be fearful" sound easy; but actually putting that into action takes some trust, faith, a lot of prayers, and patience. Sometimes, our fears hold us down, and it really takes God's mercy to release us from our fears. Just like with thankfulness, the Bible is loaded with scriptures about not holding on to fear. That makes me think that God does not want us to live in fear.

- "So do not fear, for I am with you; do not be dismayed, for I am your God. I will strengthen you and help you; I will uphold you with my righteous right hand" (Isa. 41:10).
- "When I am afraid, I put my trust in you" (Psalm 56:3).
- "Do not be anxious about anything, but in every situation, by prayer and petition, with thanksgiving, present your requests to God. And the peace of God, which transcends all understanding, will guard your hearts and your minds in Christ Jesus" (Phil. 4:6-7).

A lot of my battles with fear are fought in my mind. I tend to overthink things. I dwell on what I said in conversation, wondering if I said something wrong, worrying that I hurt someone's feelings. I worry that people will not like me for who I am, and I hold on to regrets for missing an opportunity to love someone well. I think about what words are said to me; and if they are hurtful words, they weigh on my heart. I think about them constantly and start allowing those words to paint a mental image of who I am.

Honestly, I wish I was always kind, always there for everyone. I wish I was more considerate and less selfish. I wish I was perfect, but I am not God. I do not think we should stress about every encounter we have with other humans. We should not allow their words and their heart issues to define us. We should not always have to wonder if we did things right or wrong. We Christians should be humble but not filled with self-doubt. That virtuous woman was supposed to be modest in appearance and in attitude, but she was not incapable. She showed her virtue through her actions. She was confident, hard-working, and diligent.

First Peter 5:6-7 urges us, "Humble yourselves, therefore, under God's mighty hand, that he may lift you up in due time. Cast all your anxiety on him because he cares for you." According to Dictionary.com, humble means "having a feeling of insignificance, inferiority, subservience, etc." or "low in rank, importance, status, quality."[5]

Being humble does not mean we are incapable. In fact, it means the exact opposite. We *are* capable; and because of that, we need to not try and get all that glory and attention that belongs to God. If we humble ourselves, He will exalt us. He will use us for His glory and purpose. And we can give Him all of our worries and anxieties because He cares for us (1 Peter 5:7).

Sometimes, you just have to let God take over. Trust Him for the peace that seems so hard to find. Let go of relationships that are tearing you down. Let go of the hurt that you have held onto and learn to forgive. Sometimes, you have to close doors that are allowing hurt and fear access into your life. Sometimes, you have to pray and ask God to close those impossible doors.

---

5 Dictionary.com, s.v. "Humble," accessed May 29, 2023, https://www.dictionary.com/browse/humble.

Chapter 12

Who's to Blame?

The man said, "The woman you put here with me—she gave me some fruit from the tree, and I ate it." Then the LORD God said to the woman, "What is this you have done?" The woman said, "The serpent deceived me, and I ate."

Genesis 3:12-13

In life, we often turn to the blame game. When things go wrong in our lives, we tend to look for reasons why we are struggling. Sometimes, we blame God; oftentimes, we blame others, our parents, our circumstances, and our finances; and sometimes, we blame ourselves.

Adam and Eve had this problem, too. When they messed up in the Garden of Eden, they were quick to point the blame. Adam was the first to cast blame: "Look, it's this woman you gave me." Eve pointed out the serpent and blamed him for tempting her. They did not want to own up to the fact that their hearts were not right with God and that they had made a mistake.

We all want to look good, live well, be respected, have wealth, and enjoy good health, all while getting those perfect vacation photos from the summer. We want people to look at us and know that we have it all together. We desire perfection, but that is not the world in which we live. Life is so full of ups and downs.

When my mom passed away, my family struggled with the blame game. Should we have taken her to the hospital sooner? Did taking her to the hospital make her better or worse? Did we say the right words or do the right things? Was it the doctors' faults? Was it our fault? Was it God's fault? Death takes a toll on hearts that are suddenly completely broken. We want to blame someone for the hurt.

Do things always work in cause and effect? Is everything that affects us someone's fault, neglect, or sin? Or does life just throw stones at random? I know that we live in a broken world. I guess, in a way, it is easy to say that it is all Adam and Eve's fault from the very beginning when they introduced death and pestilence into the world. But if we had been in their shoes and had the same temptations, we would likely have chosen the same thing. So, here we are in a broken and hurting world, casting stones of blame at anyone that gets in the way when we get hurt. Sometimes, life just happens. Sometimes, death takes hold of our loved ones, and there is nothing that we can do.

On the other hand, sometimes we are quick to cast stones when we have not checked our own hearts. A verse that is so often thrown in a Christian's face is, "Do not judge, or you too will be judged" (Matt. 7:1). And it is the truth, biblically. We all make mistakes and sin. As Romans 3:23 says, "For all have sinned and fall short of the glory of God." If that was not true, then we would not need a Savior. Looking inwardly at our own shortcomings lets us have more grace for others when they fall short. But Romans 2:1 reminds us, "You, therefore, have no excuse, you who pass judgment on someone else, for at whatever point you judge another, you are condemning yourself, because you who pass judgment do the same things."

Our sins may not be ones that are as "visible" as other people's sins. We tend to forget that pride is one of the top heart issues. Jesus tells the story about the Pharisee, who said, "'God, I thank you that I am not like . . . this tax collector'" (Luke 18:10). The tax collector knew his guilt and could not even look toward Heaven. He was so ashamed. He prayed to be forgiven. Jesus said that the tax collector was the one who had his heart right with God and not the other.

I do not know about you, but I know that sometimes, I need to check myself. I need to pray and ask God to show me what I am doing wrong, to reveal what wicked ways are causing separation from Him, and to ask Him to search my heart.

Sometimes, sin sneaks up on us. We do not even realize we have allowed pride, prejudice, greed, malice, or hate to burrow into our hearts. We turn a blind eye to the actions that are causing us to sin. We do not realize that we are the ones spreading gossip and lies. We think we have it all together, so we point the blame at the "sinners" when there is a conflict. If we are really good at it, we will make them look lesser, so we look good on our pedestals.

First John 1:8 says, "If we claim to be without sin, we deceive ourselves and the truth is not in us." Talk about a wake-up call! I am preaching to myself and the rest of the choir. *We are sinners.* We make mistakes. We are human. We are flawed. Proverbs 21:2 reminds us that "a person may think their own ways are right, but the LORD weighs the heart."

So, what can we do about it? Have an honest conversation with yourself and God. Dive into His Word. Meditate on the affairs of your heart. Hebrews 4:12 says, "For the word of God is alive and active. Sharper than any double-edged sword, it penetrates even to dividing soul and spirit, joints and marrow; it judges the thoughts and attitudes of the heart." It will hurt when you start fact-checking your thoughts and intents. It might sever a few joints, and you might bleed out a little bit of that pride.

I am right there with you. Truth hurts. But also, truth heals. Jesus is that Truth. So, the verse about not judging is really for a Christian to not judge an unbeliever. God should be the One convicting them of what they are doing wrong once they are saved. As unbelievers, they are not held to the same standards. We should not expect them to follow the rules of football if they are not even playing the game. God's Word is a light and a lamp. We are called to be salt and light (Matt. 5:13-16) and to lead unbelievers to Christ. But we are not called to be their judge, jury, and executioners.

If a brother or a sister in Christ offends you, then follow the rules of how to tango as fellow Christians. First, if you have issues with another Christian and they are to blame for a problem, then go to them. They may not even realize that they have offended you or caused a problem. Talk to them directly, face-to-face. I know it is hard to do, but really, most of the time, you can resolve a problem and come through on the other side as closer friends. But remember, when you are confronting someone, be kind. Be honest, be forgiving, and think about what Jesus would want you to do.

Matthew 18:15-20 gives us clear instructions on how to handle a disagreement with another believer:

> "If your brother or sister sins, go and point out their fault, just between the two of you. If they listen to you, you have won them over. But if they will not listen, take one or two others along, so that 'every matter may be established by the testimony of two or three witnesses.' If they still refuse to listen, tell it to the church; and if they refuse to listen even to the church, treat them as you would a pagan or a tax collector.

> "Truly I tell you, whatever you bind on earth will be bound in heaven, and whatever you loose on earth will be loosed in heaven.

> "Again, truly I tell you that if two of you on earth agree about anything they ask for, it will be done for them by my Father in heaven. For where two or three gather in my name, there am I with them."

It says that if they will not listen to the church on a matter, then it is as if they are an unbeliever. They do not want to own up to the blame, and that is a heart issue on their end. Just keep your own heart in check, and do not go blasting them out of selfish ambition. "Get rid of all bitterness, rage and anger, brawling and slander, along with every form of malice. Be kind and compassionate to one another, forgiving each other, just as in Christ God forgave you" (Eph. 4:31-32).

Chapter 13

Apple of My Eye

For this is what the LORD Almighty says: "After the Glorious One
has sent me against the nations that have plundered you—
for whoever touches you touches the apple of his eye—"

Zechariah 2:8

Here is a little testimony of something that I have held in my heart for a long time—something so clear that I know it was from God Himself. It gives me chills that He, the Creator of the universe, would speak so clearly to me. I had never before felt God's presence on this level. I had taken some of the teen girls from my church to a conference, but as a youth pastor's wife, I was struggling with my identity as a leader. I wanted to be there for the girls, but I did not feel qualified to actually talk to them about how valuable they were to God because I was still struggling with my own value. How could I tell another person how important they were to God as His children if I did not even know how to embrace that truth for myself?

I cannot remember who the speaker was, but the message was something that resonated with me. She said, "We are the apple of God's eye." What does that even mean? At that point in time, I had heard that phrase before in Scripture or just as a common expression, but I did not know the impact of the meaning.

The literal meaning of "apple of my eye" is talking about the reflection of yourself seen in other people's pupils. It means you are being watched so closely by someone that you can be seen in their eyes. Your very image is the central focus of that person. As the speaker explained what this expression meant, I felt in my spirit that I wanted to be the apple of God's eye. But who am I to have God love me that much? That was an impossible kind of love. I do not deserve to be anyone's focus or attention, especially not the King of kings. None of us do. We are all sinners who did not and cannot do anything to earn God's love and grace.

I went home that evening in tears because I just could not imagine that God felt that way about me. I sat all evening with that on my heart and mind. The next day at church, we had a visiting minister. He did not know that I had just poured out my heart to God about wanting to be the "apple of His eye." He did not know that I was searching for that feeling of belonging and value and identity in Christ. For all he knew, I was just another Christian woman in a church. At the end of the service, he had everyone come up to the front for prayer. I did not know the impact of this man's walk with God—that he was someone who listened and spoke with God. But when he came over to pray for me, all he said was, "*You* are the apple of God's eye."

It still gives me chills and makes me cry. The God of the universe spoke through a man to tell me who I was in Him. There is no coincidence here. Nothing else mattered at that moment more than God wanting me to know I am His. He even confirms this in Psalm 17:8: "Keep me as the apple of your eye; hide me in the shadow of your wings."

And just imagine: if God would speak to the doubts and hurts in my heart, how will He speak to your heart, dear brothers and sisters in Christ? We are all sinners, but Christ *died* for us. We are all the apples of His eyes. He loves us. We are so precious in His sight that He watches after us. We can see ourselves in the reflection of His eyes.

And with that promise, that assurance also comes as a covenant. God says, "I am this; I will do this; I am faithful. But I also want something from you. I want your love and your heart in return." He is faithful and long-suffering with us. We make mistakes, but He still loves us and gently pulls our hearts back to Him. Here is His covenant: "Keep my commands and you will live; guard my teachings as the apple of your eye" (Prov. 7:2). He wants us to keep His Word as the apple of our eyes. He wants us to meditate on His Word, to put them "on the doorframes of [our] houses" (Deut. 6:9), to love Him as much as He loves us. He wants His beloved to desire Him as much as He desires them. Oh, how I want to be His. I want to soak in His love. I want to be seen and to see His face clearly.

Chapter 14

Temptations

Blessed is the one who perseveres under trial because, having stood the test, that person will receive the crown of life that the Lord has promised to those who love him.

James 1:12

"Don't say you would never do something; you just might turn around and find yourself doing the very thing you said you wouldn't." This is a quote from one of my aunts (whom I never met). It is something she used to tell my dad growing up, and he has said it time and again to me. In his words, "It's easy to say you would never do what that other sinner is doing, but then, you sometimes find yourself in that very same situation."

On earth, we are still living in a sinful nature. We are still occupying these old bodies made up of flesh and bones, and we are still tempted by the things of this world. Just when we think we have it all together, we fall, or we fail. We do not always fall into visible sins. Sometimes, sin looks like pride, anger, or words we regret. It may show up as losing our morals, watching shows that are a "little" too risqué, have a "little" too much cursing, include a "little" black magic, show a "little" violence. We might be tempted to drink a "little" too much with our friends, or tell a "little" white lie, or accidentally take the Lord's name in vain. I know sometimes, I do not realize that I am crossing the line when I have scooted up as close to it as I can.

The Israelites had the same problem. There they were, following God across the wilderness, millions of people released from slavery, following a pillar of cloud by day and fire by night. They had Moses and God leading the camp. God was pouring out His covenant with them, telling them that if they just kept His laws and commands, He would outdo all that He had already done for them. What a promise! But then, they got to Peor.

There is an interesting story in the Bible in Numbers 22:2-25:9. Balak, one of the Moabite kings of the land, saw the Israelites coming; and he got nervous. He asked this soothsayer/priest, Balaam, to come up to the top of a mountain at Peor. He wanted Balaam to look out at the Israelites and curse his enemies so that they would be easily defeated. Balaam came (after a struggle with his talking donkey), but God only let him bless the people of Israel, not curse them.

It is a really interesting story, and I almost thought that Balaam was one of the good guys since he communed with God. He had the God of the universe speaking to Him, but he was more concerned about money than his relationship with God. The part of the story that is easily missed happens after he has finished blessing Israel. He decided to quit communing with God; he did not like that God wanted to keep blessing the Israelites because it meant he was not going to get paid by King Balak. He was going home empty-handed. So, here's where it gets interesting. He tells the king, if you just get the Israelites to join in with your people and follow after your god Baal, then God will quit blessing them. He helped Balak devise a plan to tempt the Israelites and cause them to sin. Sadly, his plan worked.

The word *Baal* just means "lord." The people of the land worshiped many gods, so there were a lot of different Baals worshiped in the Old Testament. Peor was probably just named after a place, but the word translates to "opening." So, Baal Peor would be the "lord at the opening." And it was here at Peor that the Israelites opened themselves up to problems. Sometimes, you just need a tiny crack or opening to let sin take over your life. At Peor, the people quit worshiping the one true God and decided instead to turn toward sexual immorality, thus breaking the new covenant that God had *just* made with them. How frustrating for both God and Moses! Here at Peor, God allowed a plague to break out on the people, showing His nature not only as a just God but also as a merciful God in that He stopped the plague before all of them were destroyed.

This is not a tale to take lightly, but there is hope. Temptations are common to mankind. We *all* experience them. We *all* get tempted. We *all* face those moments when some openings and cracks allow sin into our lives. The Bible says that God is faithful. He will give us opportunities to say no to those things that draw away our hearts. We have a Comforter, the Holy Spirit, Who will convict us. We have a conscience that will weigh on us when we start down the wrong path. Our sins do have consequences, but if we can withstand the temptations that pull at our hearts, we will inherit a crown of life.

We do not have to endure the temptations alone. First Corinthians 10:13 tells us, "No temptation has overtaken you except what is common to mankind. And God is faithful; he will not let you be tempted beyond what you can bear. But when you are tempted, he will also provide a way out so that you can endure it." And if we endure, He promises us the crown of life.

It is amazing that God Himself (Jesus) came to earth to live a life like ours! He experienced pain, death, hunger, sickness, sweat, body odor, and loss. He experienced growing pains, those awkward moments of making new friends, and the harder moments of making enemies. He worked a job until He was ready to start His ministry. He experienced life just like us, and most importantly, He experienced temptations. Matthew 4:1 tells us, "Then Jesus was led by the Spirit into the wilderness to be tempted by the devil." He knows how hard it is to live in this world of sin and death. He knows what it is like to be a human. And because of that experience, He gives us a way out. He gives us an example of how to resist temptations:

1. Know your Bible. Jesus quoted Scripture to Satan. He knew what the Word of God said and used it as a sword to fight back at him.

2. Watch and Pray. Jesus taught us how to pray. We need to ask God to help us resist temptation. Sometimes, we just cannot do it on our own. But God can close those openings to sin and send us help.

3. Tell Satan to leave. Like those "Just Say No" drug campaigns from the '80s, sometimes, we just need to say no to temptation. There will be people in our lives who try to pull us under and convince us to do things that will separate us from the love of God. We must stand firm and say no. Those people who try to tempt us will eventually go away. However, this can come at a cost. When you say no, you may push away friends or family. But sometimes, you have to separate yourself from relationships to walk closer to God. Matthew 6:12-13 tells us, "And forgive us our debts, as we also have forgiven our debtors. And lead us not into temptation, but deliver us from the evil one" (Matt. 6:12-13).

Praise God for His great faithfulness. He will see us through if we just put our trust and hope in him. We need the armor of God to stand. It is not easy to resist the devil. His whispers in our ears sometimes sound like our own thoughts. We might get overwhelmed by the battle, but when we have done everything in our power to resist, we just have to stand on God's Word, our solid foundation. As Matthew 26:41 says, "'Watch and pray so that you will not fall into temptation. The spirit is willing, but the flesh is weak.'"

Chapter 15

Overwhelmed

There remains, then, a Sabbath-rest for the people of God; for anyone who enters God's rest also rests from their works, just as God did from his. Let us, therefore, make every effort to enter that rest, so that no one will perish by following their example of disobedience.

Hebrews 4:9-11

I have stressed how important it is to seek after God, try to live our best for God, and teach our children to seek after God. These are all great things, but if I am being real, those are all things we try to do on our own. Rest comes when we step back from the workload of trying to do everything, stop trying to do what is in our power, and give it to God. I am not good at this. I do not like to step back from the workload and rest in God.

We all get overwhelmed. At least, I hope I am not the only one out there who gets overstimulated, overworked, and overloaded. Surely, I am not the only one who lets anxieties get the upper hand. After all, misery loves company, right?

This week was one of those weeks. My mind could not function to add or subtract numbers with my kids for their school. I had a long tutor meeting planned, homeschool co-ops to prepare for, our children's church ministry to organize, and so many things to do and places to be. The brain fog was real. If I were a cartoon character, you would see me pictured with a big, gray cloud around my head. I almost felt as though everyone who saw me could tell I was an unorganized, frizzled mess.

But in reality, nobody noticed that I was inwardly screaming out because I outwardly played the part. I made it to the places to do the things, and although I was late and frazzled, I was there. I threw makeup on and smiled. I tried to put on the front of having it together; but as soon as I made it home, I was grumpy, yelling at the kids, crying in my room, and exhausted.

Why do we let ourselves get to this point of inner cries for relief while covering it up under the obligation of keeping up with social expectations? I need rest, to sit and be still, to soak in the Holy Spirit, to sit at Jesus' feet like Mary did in Luke 10. Even God rested. He gave us an example in the Creation story. Right at the very beginning of everything, He showed us the importance of rest. God also promises to give us rest at the end of our stories When we have fought the good fight and been obedient to God, we will enter into His rest.

But what about right now, in this lifetime? What about here in the middle of the overwhelming parts of life? What is our promise for rest when it feels like we cannot make it over this mountain? Scriptures say to give it all to Jesus: "'Come to me, all you who are weary and burdened, and I will give you rest. Take my yoke upon you and learn from me, for I am gentle and humble in heart, and you will find rest for your souls. For my yoke is easy and my burden is light'" (Matt. 11:28-30).

But what does that mean? What does it mean to find rest in Jesus? Here is the reality: even though I may know the answer to the question, I struggle with applying it to my life. I know that to live a healthy life, I must eat healthy food, exercise, drink lots of water, etc. But just because I know the solution to the problem does not mean I am not stuffing my face with cookies at midnight while binge-watching a favorite show. I mean, the kids are in bed, and I finally have some time to spend with my husband. But I know that if I want more energy, I probably need to work out and keep fit. (Walking back and forth from the laundry room counts as exercise, right?) Just because we have the solution does not mean we know how to apply it.

The Holy Spirit still calls to us past the excuses and the overwhelming moments. He gently invites us to seek Him. His still, small Voice whispers for us to stop trying to be all the things for all the people and just seek Him. Just be still. "He says, 'Be still, and know that I am God; I will be exalted among the nations, I will be exalted in the earth'" (Psalm 46:10).

You would think that sitting down and being still is one of the easiest things to do, right? Doesn't everyone want a break? So, why is it so hard to stop constantly working and doing things? Why is it so hard to listen to God's voice and direction?

I think the answer to that question lies in our want to control. I want to be in charge of my life and destiny. If I sit still and wait on God, I am not charging ahead and "gettin' 'er done." Why wait on God's voice when I can apply for that job; so I can afford the car, house, clothes, and all the things I want? Why pray and trust God for a missing wallet when I can search all over the house from top to bottom? When I want something, I want it *now*; I am not good at patience. I want to do the things that are in my power to control. It is not until all is lost and things get impossible that I start looking for God. So, I work; and I work; and I work—instead of just stopping and praying, instead of breathing in the Holy Spirit and allowing His peace to enter my life. I think I have things under control when I am spiraling out of control.

But if we stop, trust, and breathe in His promise of rest, God will give it to us. He is a faithful God, even when we are unfaithful. We just need to turn back to Him. Second Chronicles 7:14-16 says:

> If my people, who are called by my name, will humble themselves and pray and seek my face and turn from their wicked ways, then I will hear from heaven, and I will forgive their sin and will heal their land. Now my eyes will be open and my ears attentive to the prayers offered in this place. I have

chosen and consecrated this temple so that my Name may
be there forever. My eyes and my heart will always be there.

Many scriptures are promises of blessings God made to the
Israelites during their history. However, God is a faithful, merciful,
compassionate God, Who opened His covenants to both the Gentiles
and the Jews. God had promised the Israelites blessings if they turned
their lives around and sought after Him. And those blessings and promises
apply to us as well!

Jonah is a prophet in the Bible who was angry with God. He was
unhappy that God had not destroyed the wicked people of Nineveh.
Jonah complains a lot throughout his book, but in his complaint to
God, he is ironically telling us how awesome our God is. Jonah showed
his human nature and wanted those people to get what they deserved.
He was not showing love.

In Jonah 4:2, "He prayed to the LORD, 'Isn't this what I said, LORD,
when I was still at home? That is what I tried to forestall by fleeing
to Tarshish. I knew that you are a gracious and compassionate God,
slow to anger and abounding in love, a God who relents from sending
calamity." But how awesome is it that God does not give people what
they deserve? He shows mercy and grace to us. God eagerly turns away
from destruction and death because He loves us.

Our God is compassionate; He is not a Respecter of persons. He
loves both the Jew and the Gentile. God adopted us into His family.
So now, we can receive His promise of eternal life and all His other
covenants, like His promise of rest.

Chapter 16

Loving Deep

"Do not seek revenge or bear a grudge against anyone among your people, but love your neighbor as yourself. I am the LORD.'"

Leviticus 19:18

During the moments of quiet, this is when I think about all the missed opportunities of the day. The kids are finally in bed after a long day of busy. We have been running here and there all day long. I am sitting at the table reflecting on the day and everything I did, whether right or wrong. We had a goodbye party for our local librarian, who is moving on to bigger and better things. There is a sadness in saying "so long" to someone who has influenced my kids for the last ten years. She was not even my best friend or someone I would call to help me with an issue close to home. I did not confide personal things to her; but she was someone my kids and I loved, respected, and enjoyed being around.

I have other friends and family going through battles I could not even imagine, and then there are those I will not see again until I see them in Heaven. My heart aches as I think of people leaving my life. I do not do well with goodbyes. I am awkward and struggle enough with hellos, but goodbyes are much more difficult. I unintentionally let people fade away as life inevitably changes. I get busy and do not make as much time for phone calls, visits, or meet-ups. Usually, it is mutual as our lives move in different directions. I do not want people leaving my life; but sometimes, friends and family are just there for the moment, a chapter in this book we call life.

I wish I had the right words to say during the goodbye moments instead of waiting until the opportunity has passed. Yet here I am, sitting in the quiet stillness of the evening and going over the words and heartfelt thoughts that were left unspoken. I wish I had said the words "I love you" and let them know they touched my heart in ways they could not have imagined. Why do words of love and friendship remain unspoken on my tongue? The more goodbyes I experience, the more I wish I had the right words.

We are even commanded by Jesus to love. In Matthew 22:37-39, "Jesus replied: *'Love the Lord your God with all your heart and with all your soul and with all your mind.'* This is the first and greatest commandment. And the second is like it: *'Love your neighbor as yourself.'*"

God calls us to love others. We should not love quietly; that kind of love leaves silently and goes unnoticed by those who need to see the love in action and hear the words of affirmation. Instead, we should love unconditionally, boldly, loudly, and unapologetically. So, why is it so hard to say goodbye, thank you, and I love you? It may be because it opens us up to being vulnerable.

Love is such a complex word. It is not always deep. Sometimes, people I barely know will casually tell me that they love me in passing. It is a quick and relatively meaningless "see ya later; love ya!" When this happens, it always catches me off guard because then I have to think about how deep *my* love actually is for that person. And if it is not a deep love, saying it back feels fake and insincere. That does not mean I do not like that person or feel affection toward them; I do not tend to express "love" so casually. If I am going to tell someone that I love them, it is usually heartfelt and genuine. But that is where the vulnerability comes in. If I open myself up to expressing that love, I am opening myself up to questioning whether they love me back.

It is natural to have certain people we love and hold closer to our hearts than others. Jesus was not afraid to show people He loved them. He showed His love through His actions of healing, caring, and teaching. Jesus had compassion for the hurting and the sick. He loved His neighbor to the point of dying for them. Yet Jesus also showed special love to His closest friends. He had a community of believers and disciples who got most of His time, affection, and attention.

In John 13: 1, we read, "It was just before the Passover Festival. Jesus knew that the hour had come for him to leave this world and go to the Father. Having loved his own who were in the world, he loved them to the end." Jesus loved His disciples and said goodbye to them in one of the sweetest ways. He showed it through washing their feet. Jesus, the King of the universe, humbled Himself and did what was considered a servant's chore to show them how love should work. He got down to their level and told them they were special to him. During His ministry, Jesus did not hold back from correcting His disciples when they made terrible decisions. He spoke love to them—the deep, truthful, raw love from the heart. He was vulnerable; He was real.

Still, that love did not prevent one of His disciples from turning around and betraying Jesus and giving Him over for money. Then, the other disciple, who loved Jesus, turned and denied Jesus to save his own life. These were some of His best friends; yet in the end, they all ran. God knows vulnerability; He knows how hard it is to love deeply. Yet He was willing to be vulnerable, even to the point of death. And that is what He asks of us in Matthew 5:43-48:

> "You have heard that it was said, 'Love your neighbor and hate your enemy.' But I tell you, love your enemies and pray for those who persecute you, that you may be children of your Father in heaven. He causes His sun to rise on the evil and the good, and sends rain on the righteous and the unrighteous. If you love those who love you, what reward will you get? Are not even the tax collectors doing that? And if you greet only your own people, what are you doing more than others? Do not even pagans do that? Be perfect, therefore, as your heavenly Father is perfect."

"What is love?" This question seems like it should have a simple answer, but it is much more nuanced than just being kind or caring. For example, Jesus says we should love our neighbor as ourselves. What does that mean? What if I do not even like my neighbor? What if they hurt me or wronged me? What if they have said words that have torn me down and made me feel like dirt? Jesus said even then, you are supposed to love them when people are at their most unlovable.

When you cannot change them, cannot stand them, cannot help them, that is when you tell them you love them and then pray for them. Then you turn it over to God and let Him change them, help them, and stand with them. I am not saying you must hang out with your worst enemies and try to be their best friends. But instead of holding that hatred in your heart, let forgiveness and acceptance take its place.

Is that always easy? No, people can be vile. They can steal your joy, hope, and faith if you let them. But they can also be kind, considerate, and loving. You can easily connect with some people, but with others, it is like pulling teeth to talk to them because they grate against your nerves. People are so complex and interesting. But in the end, they are just like you and me. We all face struggles, shame, anxiety, temptation, pride, and foolishness. We all go through the motions. We all try to live according to what is good in our own eyes, but that does not always align with what is good in God's eyes.

Love—the raw, real, vulnerable, forgiving, patient, gentle, humble, and unstoppable kind of love—is almost impossible to find and even more challenging to give because we are human. We are selfish, sinful, conceited people who have difficulty letting go of our pride and prejudice. We struggle with loving someone through their circumstances when it gets inconvenient. We get our feelings hurt and allow our hatred to push others from our lives. But that is not what God wants from us. He wants us to get down deep in the dirt with other humans and still show them love—to push aside our grievances and allow Him to work in their lives.

Love is the most important thing. We read this in 1 Corinthians 13:1-8:

> If I speak in the tongues of men or of angels, but do not have love, I am only a resounding gong or a clanging cymbal. If I have the gift of prophecy and can fathom all mysteries and all knowledge, and if I have a faith that can move mountains, but do not have love, I am nothing. If I give all I possess to the poor and give over my body to hardship that I may boast, but do not have love, I gain nothing. Love is patient, love is kind. It does not envy, it does not boast, it is not proud. It does not dishonor others, it is not self-seeking, it is not easily angered, it keeps no record of wrongs. Love does not delight in evil but rejoices with the truth. It always protects, always trusts, always hopes, always perseveres. Love never fails.

Sometimes, when I know someone is going through heartbreak, I want to avoid eye contact. I do not want to meet their eyes because I know if I do, I am likely to break down and cry. I have great empathy and do not want to feel their pain. At least, I tell myself it is for their sake, but it is just cowardice. I do not want to take the time to sit and let them experience the hurt because it is painful; but often, that is what is needed. They need someone to look them in the eyes and say it is okay to cry. It is okay to hurt when you are grieving. It is okay to shed a few tears when you are exhausted, overwhelmed, or even excited and happy. Tears are God's design, a way to set those emotions free.

In John 11, we see that Jesus cared so much about Mary and Martha that He wept. A whole verse of the Bible was dedicated to that precious moment. He did not blink away from their hurt. Jesus knew He could fix it, but He also knew what they were experiencing. John 11:35 is the shortest verse of the Bible, yet it speaks volumes as to the nature of our God. He was not afraid to say goodbye. He embraced the awkward hello by changing lives in one conversation. He got on a deep level with people. He was not apprehensive about listening to people, experiencing their pain, and loving them. He was not afraid to get in the middle of the hurt, the joy, and the life of those He loved.

I started this chapter with how hard it is to show love to the lovable, and I am finishing with how hard it is to show love to the *un*lovable. We need to do both. We are the hands and feet of Jesus, called to reflect His love for even the shameless, obnoxious, and vilest of people. Through our efforts, we become light. We point them toward Someone even greater, Who loves them at their worst. It is not always easy to show real love. I often fail when I try to be loving. Yet I desire to be salt, light, hope, and love. I want to show the world Jesus. And thankfully, He loves me even when I fail at that. He loves all of us at our selfish, sinful, worst moments and calls us on to a deeper walk with him.

Chapter 17

Joy to the World

You turned my wailing into dancing; you removed my sackcloth and clothed me with joy, that my heart may sing your praises and not be silent. LORD my God, I will praise you forever.

Psalm 30:11-12

Joy! How did I forget one of the essential benefits of serving God? I keep talking about all the hard, worthwhile things but not with the mindset of why it matters. Even in the middle of hardships, the apostles counted it all *joy*. Serving our risen Savior is worthwhile because He gives us love, *joy*, peace, patience, kindness, goodness, and faithfulness.

Joy comes in when you stop looking at life from the perspective of how you can get more, be more, gain more importance, and be praised and instead start looking at it with a perspective of what you can do to help others, serve God, be less, and praise God.

Joy is so much more than happiness. God wants that for us, too. He gives us the gift of laughter, fun, happiness, and sunny days; but He also lets the rain fall on both the just and unjust. But joy is where you can still praise God when life is hard and there is sorrow, sickness, and death. Even through the unfaceable circumstances of life, you can still have joy in your heart. What a gift!

He gives us abundantly above what we could ask or imagine. We can find joy in a sunrise, in a simple moment watching our children learn, in the sweet exchange of a smile with a stranger. So many precious moments of this life can bring us simple joy if we know where our joy comes from and if we know the Joy-maker. Because the Father loves us, we can experience true joy.

> "As the Father has loved me, so have I loved you. Now remain in my love. If you keep my commands, you will remain in my love, just as I have kept my Father's commands and remain in his love. I have told you this so that my joy may be in you and that your joy may be complete. My command is this: Love each other as I have loved you. Greater love has no one than this: to lay down one's life for one's friends. You are my friends if you do what I command. I no longer call you servants, because a servant does not know his master's business. Instead, I have called you friends, for everything that I learned from my Father I have made known to you. You did not choose me, but I chose you and appointed you so that you might go and bear fruit—fruit that will last—and so that whatever you ask in my name the Father will give you. This is my command: Love each other" (John 15:9-17).

If we love others, obey His commands, and remain in His love, then we will have joy—not just happiness, but a joy that is overflowing! Jesus said He no longer calls us enslaved people but His friends, His family. He chose us and wants us to have His joy. It is not by anything we could do but by His sacrifice on the cross that we can even come into His presence. He fought for and bought us with His very life. And now, He wants to give us above and beyond our wildest imaginations. He wants to provide us with the sheer joy of life.

Joy is not something that is produced by having an easy life. While God does promise to help us through this life, He also tells us that it will be hard. We live in a broken world full of broken people. We came from dust, like grass withering away, and will turn back to dust. At its most basic, this life is simple: we eat, sleep, and die. We came into this world with nothing, and we will leave this world with nothing.

The book of Ecclesiastes speaks of everything being meaningless, life being hard, and working to get somewhere in life, only to then die. But God calls us to look for more out of this life. It says that life is meaningless without God. But with God at your side, you can have wisdom, knowledge, happiness, and joy. God is the difference between a joyless life and a joy-filled, meaningful life.

In Ecclesiastes 2:24-26, Solomon writes:

> A person can do nothing better than to eat and drink and find satisfaction in their own toil. This too, I see, is from the hand of God, for without him, who can eat or find enjoyment? To the person who pleases him, God gives wisdom, knowledge and happiness, but to the sinner he gives the task of gathering and storing up wealth to hand it over to the one who pleases God. This too is meaningless, a chasing after the wind.

What really matter are the people we affect, the choices we make, the ones we love, the moments we experience, the memories we make, and the souls we save. Joy comes from the moments between all the toil and sweat when we let God be our Guide and Deliverer.

The apostles lived in poverty, were supported by the churches, and worked hard to share the Gospel. They faced hunger, pain, embarrassment, torture, and even death. Christians in the modern churches of America do not face suffering or death for our beliefs. We might meet times of hunger and poverty if we seek a life of serving God, but the church usually supports the ministry. But embarrassment *is* something we face.

We live in a society that will cut down a Christian for things like cancel culture, viewpoints that feel condemning, or anything that goes against the modern sense of political correctness. But I am going off on a rabbit trail. The point is we will face some hardships, too, but they are not likely going to be as physically intense as what the early Christians endured. But those Christians counted it all joy to fall into various hardships. They found joy in seeing God provide for their needs. These believers found joy when they were beaten or thrown into prison because they were God's hands and feet. And we can find joy in God providing for our needs. We can find joy when serving the Master and walking on the path He leads us down.

Jesus compares the love the Father has for us with the love a father has for his child. You would have to be a messed-up lowlife if you gave your child a rock when they wanted bread or a snake instead of a fish dinner. In this passage in Matthew 7, Jesus shows us that if a human father (just a regular, old person with flaws and sins) is willing to show love to his children, then how much more abundantly will God show love to His children? He wants His children to be well-fed, happy, content, and blessed and to live life more abundantly. He wants His children to have joy. God is so good to His children.

King David also knew about God's provision. In Psalm 37:25, David says, "I was young and now I am old, yet I have never seen the righteous forsaken or their children begging bread."

So even in times of financial lows, God will see us through. We will face hardship; we live in a broken world. But life is not meaningless. If we trust and serve him, we will live a joyous life full of His abundance. He is our Provider, our Joy-bringer.

If you have not read through Ecclesiastes, I suggest you do. It may be a bit dark in its outlook on life, chock-full of "life is meaningless" statements, but the book is also full of wisdom. Every chapter begins with King Solomon trying to find the meaning of life through his power, strength, time, and wealth. He says that we can try our hardest to build, work, grow, make money, and live in the pleasures of this life; but without God, it does not bring us joy. Politicians are corrupt, and rulers are evil and dishonest. Greed never has enough—the more wealth you have, the more fake friends you will have to spend your money. He has a bleak outlook on life, but he concludes the book with what matters—living a life that pleases God. Both the "good" and "bad" people of this world die. It is about balance, contentment, and trusting God to see you through this life.

Ecclesiastes 12:13-14 tells us that the fear of God is what is most important in our lives: "Now all has been heard; here is the conclusion of the matter: Fear God and keep his commandments, for this is the duty of all mankind. For God will bring every deed into judgment, including every hidden thing, whether it is good or evil.

I feel like this entire chapter did not sound very "joyous." I referenced a book of the Bible that has a bleak outlook on life, but that is where God comes in and turns things around. He finds us in the middle of the everyday grind and sweat, the chaos of getting through a busy day. When you are writing a book and have a child demanding breakfast, are struggling to pay the bills, are toiling over a broken-down washer, want to give up for the day—when things are just hard (my favorite word of this book)—that is when joy comes in.

Joy is when you smell roses and honeysuckle after the rain or when a friend comes over and comforts you when you are experiencing tragedy and grief. Joy is when God shows up with unexpected finances to cover that bill or when the pain of a headache washes away into relief again. When you get through the tough seasons, that is when you experience joy. How else would you know what joy is without the hard? That is the kicker. We go through this life on a balance between tough, hard, and impossible things; and God sees us through to the other side—the rainbow after the rain, the summer after the winter. As it says in Ecclesiastes 3:1, "There is a time for everything." We will go through things in this life. But real joy—not just the happiness of a moment, but the deep joy of our Savior that rests quietly down in our soul—is the joy that sees us through.

Chapter 18

Growing Up

*When I was a child, I talked like a child, I thought like a child,
I reasoned like a child. When I became a man, I put the ways of
childhood behind me.*

1 Corinthians 13:11

I was reading an old diary entry the other day. I tried (somewhat successfully) to keep a journal when I was a kid. I have a few scattered entries from when I was between eight to twelve years old. I wrote about two entries a year; so it was short, little records of significant gaps in my life. It was strange to look back at what eight-year-old me thought and felt versus what twelve-year-old me wrote down.

When I was eight, every entry ended with, "It was a good day. I had fun!" And by the time I was twelve, it was, "I want to do things my own way, be something important; and my parents are ruining my life." Why do we lose our sweet, joyous, carefree ways? Why do we go through the growing-up process with growing away from the simple things that bring us joy?

Jesus told us to have childlike faith. It is easy to believe in God with childlike faith when you are a child. But as you grow up, people and life tend to have a way of skewing your view of God. It is hard to trust Him completely as you start growing up and experiencing more of life—work, car trouble, peer pressure, heartache, financial struggles, pain, death, and loss. Life has a way of stretching and morphing us from children to adults.

I can genuinely say that this year I felt more "grown-up" than I have ever felt before. Much of this is due to loss, change, and God working on my heart. I told a friend the other day that I felt like an adult for the first time this year. I am a thirty-something wife and mom to four children, have worked a job, went to college, and own a home; but none of that made me feel like I was grown. I still called home and asked my parents for advice, babysitting, recipes, help with mechanical issues, etc. I still had my safety net to fall back on. So, my "growing up" the last few years has been due to loss. Now, instead of calling to tell my parents all my troubles and have them help me through this life, my dad will call me, and I try to give him advice. We have a different, stronger, rawer, more open, and more honest relationship. Yet as "adult" as I currently feel, if my mom walked through the door, I would long to curl up in her lap, hold her, and listen as she read me a book.

I have a great example of a godly woman through my mother but also an example of living flawed. She was not perfect. She made mistakes and choices that hurt her children; yet she taught us who God is, made sacrifices for us, and loved us deeply. My children need me to be that strong, loving, caring woman for them. So, here I am, growing up. It is not always fun and not always easy, but it is worth it. I am an "adult" with the heart and mind of a sixteen-year-old girl trying to grasp my purpose in this life. I am trying to find and hold onto the simple, beautiful, carefree things of God while juggling dishes, diapers, teaching, training, sickness, basketball, marriage, ministry, etc.

As I mature, I need to grow in my faith. The Bible talks about immature Christians, still children or newborn babes in their walk with God. Hebrews 5:12-14 says, "In fact, though by this time you ought to be teachers, you need someone to teach you the elementary truths of God's word all over again. You need milk, not solid food! Anyone who lives on milk, being still an infant, is not acquainted with the teaching about righteousness. But solid food is for the mature, who by constant use have trained themselves to distinguish good from evil."

These Christians need the milk of the Word. Instead of learning what God's Word says for themselves, they are spoon-fed by the church's pastors. We are supposed to "grow in the . . . knowledge of our Lord and Savior" (2 Peter 3:18). We are supposed to have faith in God, walk the walk, and talk the talk. So how do we grow in our relationship with God? How do we grow in our faith and our knowledge? I guess it starts with a willing heart. It begins with reading the Word of God. It starts with prayer. Most importantly, it starts with giving it all over to God.

God is the One Who helps us to grow. He brings people into our lives to help water us and encourage us. And in turn, as we grow, He uses us to water and encourage other believers. That is why he tells us not to give up "meeting together" (Heb. 10:25). We need each other, and we need God at the very core of our lives.

If you want to grow in any relationship, you need to know what the other person is like. It starts with communication. If you do not talk to your husband or wife, you will not be married for long. Or at least, you will not be married to someone you know. The same is true with God. You have to communicate by praying, being still, listening, and soaking up what He has to say daily. I am not a Bible scholar. I am not going to pretend that I have answers to the deep questions of life, the denominational differences in churches, or the big doctrinal debates. But I can tell you that I have read through the entire Bible about ten times. That is not saying much, but it is consistency and growth.

I am thankful for a modern society that offers the Bible at our fingertips. I use a Bible app on my phone that reminds me to read the Word daily and offers many devotionals on almost any mental, spiritual, or emotional struggle that one might be going through. Yet I need the answers. I see things through a curtain, waiting for God to reveal them to me. As I search His Word, I learn new things every day. I may have read something twenty times. But "the word of God is alive and active. Sharper than any double-edged sword" (Heb. 4:12). It lives and breathes the knowledge I need at the moment. While I have not immersed myself in God's Word as much as I wish, I am still growing.

But in the middle of all this growth, Jesus says we are not supposed to lose our childlike faith. "And he said: 'Truly I tell you, unless you change and become like little children, you will never enter the kingdom of heaven'" (Matt. 18:3). We are not supposed to let the difficult things of this world harden us. That is the way God designed it. If Adam and Eve had not made mistakes in the garden, if they had trusted God completely, they would have remained children. They would have kept that childlike reliance on Him for all their needs and wants. But they did not listen; they rebelled. Like teenagers, they needed to stretch new muscles and find their path. But God gave them the ability to make those decisions. They made the wrong decisions, but God did not abandon them; He promised redemption.

Chapter 19

Stay Humble and Set Boundaries

When pride comes, then comes disgrace,
but with humility comes wisdom.

Proverbs 11:2

My youngest daughter, Maisie, sat in the hallway with tears streaming down her face, sobbing for me to come to her aid. As the youngest child, she has inherited the "baby-of-the-family" mentality that everything needs to go her way; and today, it just was not going her way. The older kids were having a grand, old time playing with toys. She was welcome to join them; but instead, she tried to be the boss of the place, and they kicked her out of the room.

So, there she was, crying that she did not get her way. She wanted me to take over, to rescue her, and to make *them* let *her* have her way. But that is not how things work. I told her she needed to play by their rules and join nicely. Instead of playing with the kids, she spent an hour crying until they got bored and ran off to watch a show. She missed her opportunity to play with the kids because she could not bring herself to take a lesser role in the game. There it was—pride rearing its ugly head in my four-year-old daughter. And just like pride always does, it came with bitter ramifications.

Pride wells itself up inside of all of us. It tells us we have the correct answers, that we are the ones who deserve something, who have it all together. It says we are better, wiser, wealthier, etc. Unfortunately, when we let our pride take over, we often miss out on the relationship we could have had with someone. Instead of playing with her siblings at her favorite pretend game, Maisie spent the hour sitting alone, loudly crying because she did not get her way. She has to learn to get along, share, and play fair.

Unfortunately, she is not the only one to get kicked by pride this week. Like daughter, like mother. I spent an hour after a phone call with my dad crying because I wanted the holiday plans for Thanksgiving to go my way. I wanted to take the lead and have everyone come to my house. My dad's life has been strange since my mom passed away, and it seemed like my home would be the perfect middle ground. Sure, some of it was that I wanted to show off my home, my cooking, and my hosting abilities. Other parts of it were that I wanted a place where I felt safe and in control. Instead, my plans were shot down. I felt a bit like a fool and ended up sobbing alone after the phone call because I did not get my way.

Just like Maisie, I need to learn to get along and play. I must let go of my selfish pride and ambition and love people for who they are. They might not fit my social or economic ladder, and their way of life might not be what I consider the best. But instead of being a judge, juror, and often executioner by just writing off people, maybe I could learn to let go of pride and love someone for who they are, what they think and believe, looking past the wrongdoings and appreciating their good qualities. Instead of trying to be the boss, I could enjoy what is humbly put before me and hope for the best. I do not want to miss out on the few years with my dad that I may have left because I thought I could do Thanksgiving better and wrote him out of my life for not giving me the opportunity. So, the holidays are undecided, but regardless of how they turn out, I need to maintain humility as I navigate through family and relationships.

Humility is not a word that means "roll over and get out of the way." It does not mean you should feel like you are less of a person than someone else. To be humble is not the same thing as being a loser. Do you know who the humblest person out there was? Jesus. He, the God of the universe, came and was born just like us—a naked, crying baby wrapped in all the nasty gunk of childbirth. He was born to parents who did not have much. Joseph worked as a carpenter, an everyday craftsman position that probably did not pay much. Mary raised her children as all good Jewish mothers did. It does not mention her being a graphic designer or photographer making a bunch of money on the side.

Jesus grew up and started a ministry, where He befriended fishermen, sinners, sick, and poor. He picked the rough, overlooked, unloved to be in His inner circle. Jesus was not born in a palace like the King that He is. Instead, He grew up ordinary, just like you and me. Jesus could have lived like as God on earth but instead washed His disciples' feet to show them how to be humble. He is our example of how to live.

While He walked in humility, Jesus never talked about Himself as less of a person. He did not beat himself up or act like He had low self-esteem. Jesus knew Who He was—His power and ability—yet He decided to be humble and give others a chance to shine. He allowed the poor and sinners to sit at His table and eat with him. He allowed Martha to serve Him and Mary to sit at His feet. He gave them all ways to contribute and exist around Him, where they could be at their best. Jesus was always teaching them how to be better, yet not beating them up for not being perfect.

He also did not let them sit in sin. He forgave them but told them to "go now and leave your life of sin" (John 8:11). He changed, loved, and gave them better lives; but He did not enable them. He did not say it was okay to continue to live as a tax collector cheating the poor or as an adulterous woman, but He gave them a second chance and showed them a better life.

Pride, anger, and frustration can make a person feel disconnected from others. It is hard to swallow accusations when you do not feel you are to blame. It is hard to say sorry when you know the other person was in the wrong—especially after you apologize to try and create peace, and they decide that you are the one to blame. People can be manipulative and just plain difficult. It is okay to step away from a situation if toxic traits put you in a place of depression or anger or if it is affecting your children and your life. Sometimes, you have to remove yourself from the problem. But keep humble; be kind; show love and forgiveness; and be real, raw, and honest. Honest conversations are so hard, they can hurt immensely, but they can also bring healing.

Maybe someone needs to hear why you are stepping out of their lives so they can re-evaluate how they are treating you. If they will not listen, bring in a friend or counselor to talk things through. If that does not fix the problem, then you are in the right at that point to move on. Stepping away does not mean you should stop loving that person or to quit praying for them. While you cannot change anyone or force them to see things from your perspective, God can work on hard hearts.

We are given clear instructions in Matthew 18:15-17 on how to handle difficult relationships:

> "If your brother or sister sins, go and point out their fault, just between the two of you. If they listen to you, you have won them over. But if they will not listen, take one or two others along, so that 'every matter may be established by the testimony of two or three witnesses.' If they still refuse to listen, tell it to the church; and if they refuse to listen even to the church, treat them as you would a pagan or a tax collector."

Relationships are one of the most challenging things in life. People are not always easy to get along with. Being vulnerable around someone who may hurt you is a considerable risk we have to take in this world. Friends and family do not always fit that perfect picture of what you expect from them. And to be fair, maybe you should not have such high expectations of others. Sometimes, they have personality traits, beliefs, or attitudes that are difficult to deal with. That is okay; their life is their own to control and between them and God. However, their lives should not spill that hurt, anger, and sin over into yours. So, if they are negatively affecting your life and some distance is needed, set some boundaries.

Boundaries are an essential part of life. People are constantly pushing boundaries; so, when you do not have any, you can just get run over. If someone wants to be a part of your life, that is great! Show up and be a part. If they do not, then it is up to you to decide how much effort you want to put into keeping a one-sided relationship. Just remember that God gave us grace and undeserved mercy and expects the same of us. While it is easy to write people out of our lives, the harder, holier task might be turning the other cheek and continuing to show up for those who cannot pay us back with their time and love.

I am going to put myself on the line here. Sometimes, I expect my family to show up and be a part of my life when I do not put effort into being a part of theirs. I do not spend a lot of time with my siblings. I call them every few months, and they reach out to me with the same effort. We all have lives, jobs, families, friends, and social circles; and keeping up is hard to do. Not only that, but life choices, politics, and religion separate us from getting along perfectly. Holidays have always been the time that my family would get together; but if I have yet to make an effort to keep up with them, then why should I expect them to put their family into my picture of what a holiday looks like? Here is a hint: I should not.

I am learning to accept that it is okay. Traditions change; families morph; children grow; people move; and sometimes, you have to live and breathe with the changing seasons. Life moves on, and trying to hold onto a life that is no longer there will put you in a state of depression. Listen to the wisdom of Solomon in Ecclesiastes 7:10: "Do not say, 'Why were the old days better than these?' For it is not wise to ask such questions."

This chapter is being written during the holidays when I am far from having it together. Roses and honeysuckle were in the spring, with the promise of new life, sunshine, and sweet summer on the horizon. Here on Thanksgiving week, fall is turning to winter. The weather is beginning to feel cold and bleak. I am closer to God than I was at the beginning of this year, yet His promises feel harder to obtain.

This year is about the cycle of life, emotions, change, and growth. There are seasons—physical ones, obviously, but also spiritual and emotional ones. As fall turns to winter, I am feeling the grief of loss. But even in this, there is a promise. "There is a time for everything, and a season for every activity under heaven" (Eccl. 3:1). God's promise to us is that seasons will change. Just hold on and do not be weary in well-doing (Gal. 6:9). There are rewards for making it through the seasons.

There is a time for everything, and a season for every activity under the heavens:

> *a time to be born and a time to die,*
> *a time to plant and a time to uproot,*
> *a time to kill and a time to heal,*
> *a time to tear down and a time to build,*
> *a time to weep and a time to laugh,*
> *a time to mourn and a time to dance,*
> *a time to scatter stones and a time to gather them,*
> *a time to embrace and a time to refrain from embracing,*
> *a time to search and a time to give up,*
> *a time to keep and a time to throw away,*
> *a time to tear and a time to mend,*
> *a time to be silent and a time to speak,*
> *a time to love and a time to hate,*
> *a time for war and a time for peace.*
>
> Ecclesiastes 3:1-8

Thank God we have seasons in our lives; but just like the physical seasons of the earth, they are temporary. There are breaks from the hard things to enjoy the easy stuff. There is a God Who loves us and walks us through difficult times. Like a tree, we are planted by the water (Psalm 1:3). He promised that as long as the seasons exist, the earth is here. He is not finished with us yet. He will water us, feed us, warm us in the sunlight, and rest us in the winter. We will shed our coats of many colors like autumn; we have the promise of new life like spring. We grow like well-watered trees, pushing off the vines that entangle us, growing ever stronger, rooting ourselves deeper into His Word. He prunes us, and sometimes, it hurts. But eventually, if we hold on to God, we will be strong, tall trees producing fruit. As Genesis 8:22 promises, "'As long as the earth endures, seedtime and harvest, cold and heat, summer and winter, day and night will never cease.'"

Chapter 20

For They Will Be Comforted

Blessed are those who mourn, for they will be comforted.

Matthew 5:4

I was sitting in my car on a busy day, and my thoughts returned to missing my mom. Her soul is gone on to be with Jesus, but her body sits in an unmarked grave—the kind of place where people who were unloved or unknown might reside. My mom was loved and known, yet bills and life took precedence over a gravestone.

I talked to God. I tend to do this when I get moments of quiet alone time in the car. I tell Him all my worries, thoughts, and problems while He listens. Although I *know* He hears my prayers, I do not always feel like He is present nor expect a response or an answer. I know my faith is weak, and sometimes, I need reminders of His presence.

As I was driving and chatting with God, I never expected the deep things of my heart to be spoken to so clearly. I told him I wished I had the extra money to pay for a gravestone. We had given her a proper funeral, and she was buried; but a headstone was not affordable after all the costs and life changes with her death. I wanted a place to remember her. The last time we visited her grave, we stood around what we thought was the right spot and hoped we were putting flowers on the right site, not the person next to hers. It felt silly and a little awkward. As I stood over the plot of land near where her body was

121

buried, I wanted to know that she was there, remembered and loved. From a Christian perspective, I know that it is only her body there, and her spirit and soul are with Him. I guess I want a place to see her name, grieve, and bring my children to remember.

It had been two years left undone—not because we did not want it done but because it is hard to have extra money for anyone living paycheck to paycheck. Gravestones are expensive. My dad did not have that extra money, but he felt it was his responsibility. He was open to being loaned the money to get it done, but I never seemed to have the extra money. My siblings might have had extra, but they did not want to overstep and make my dad feel bad. So, it became something that was pushed to the backburners of our lives.

I told God that I would like to be able to use whatever extra money we have this coming tax season to pay for it. I reminded Him that most of our tax refund money is used to pay for our kids' homeschool co-op tuition; so it would take some juggling, but I would like to be able to afford both. How would it all work out? It would never get done with my ability and my timing. I prayed that He would work it out and that we would eventually have that extra money. It was not even so much a request to God as it was me telling Him where I was in regards to my inability and my desire to have it happen.

Here is where it gets good. Here is where I have chills. James 1:17 tells us, "Every good and perfect gift is from above, coming down from the Father of the heavenly lights, who does not change like shifting shadows." I arrived back home, forgot my conversation with God, and went to bed. After all, those were all worries and problems for another day when I could do something about them.

The next morning, I checked my phone. I typically take care of our finances, so I randomly looked at our bank account to see what bills went out. It said there was a pending deposit of a thousand dollars. That was weird, and I knew it *had* to be a mistake. It was probably a bank error, since it was the weekend. I went all day without thinking about it. We had a busy day at church putting on a Christmas nativity play, and I did not have time to worry about it. Later that evening, after everything had settled down and I had the kids in bed, I decided to check my email to see if I had any messages from my bank and hopefully figure out why it had that pending amount.

I had an email message that said the sender was my older brother. I called him to ask what that was for and why he was sending me money. He told me that he wanted to help us as a family. It was Christmas, and he had felt led to send us some extra money to help with bills or presents for the kids. I immediately remembered the conversation with God from the day before. Through my brother's gift, God had provided just what was needed to pay for the gravestone.

I told my brother that he had just answered a prayer and asked if I could use it for a headstone. He said he could have used that money to pay for it himself, but as I said before, it would have been overstepping my dad. I hung up, and my heart praised God. I could not stop the tears from flowing. I had not even realized how important this was to me.

The following day, I called my dad. I told him that we had the extra money. He got to do all the footwork of checking around to see what needed to be done to get one ordered. He felt like he was able to honor his wife, and I felt like I was a part of it, even though God blessed us with money that was not ours. God answered a prayer that only He knew was weighing on my heart. What a Christmas present!

Had God worked it out around tax season, I may have forgotten my prayer. I would have discredited Him from being the Provider of my needs. I would have been prideful and thought I was the one to fix the problem. I would have made my dad feel bad by taking charge. Instead, I am humbled and amazed at God's provision and ability to work out things precisely as needed.

God's timing is perfect. At a time when my heart was turning toward grief over the holidays, He gave me the gift that I needed to know that He was there looking out for my heart. He comforts us when we are grieving. He gives us strength through this journey of life.

Chapter 21

Standing on God's Word

"The kingdom of heaven is like treasure hidden in a field. When a man found it, he hid it again, and then in his joy went and sold all he had and bought that field. Again, the kingdom of heaven is like a merchant looking for fine pearls. When he found one of great value, he went away and sold everything he had and bought it."

Matthew 13:44-46

It is easy to say you are a Christian. But living up to God's Word is impossible. "For all have sinned and fall short of the glory of God" (Rom. 3:23). I go through phases where I think I have it all together. Life is lining up; kids are healthy; and positive changes are happening. Life is looking good! But God does not like us to stay comfortable for too long because then we forget that He is the Provider of all good things, and we stop being dependent on Him. Too often, I get caught up in the comfortable and forget Who my Source is.

This week, my faith and stance on my beliefs were questioned. I was asked to be a part of something that I do not feel lines up with God's Word, to turn a blind eye to something I believe is a sin, and to just accept it as normal. To go along with the request would be easy. It would not ruffle any feathers. But to oppose meant possibly losing someone I care about deeply. Honestly, it felt like a lose-lose scenario. Sometimes, we have to stand firm on our values and beliefs—even when it is hard, even when it hurts, and even when it feels like a loss.

My mother-in-law said that Christians today are standing too close to the world in an attempt to show God's love, but God is not of this world. If we do not stand for our beliefs, then how are we any different? Not everyone has the same views on things in this life. What is a sin for me might be okay for another. But the One Who really decides what is sin is God. We must line up with what His Word tells us is true and be willing to lose everything in the process. Jesus said, "'If anyone comes to me and does not hate father and mother, wife and children, brothers and sisters—yes, even their own life—such a person cannot be my disciple. And whoever does not carry their cross and follow me cannot be my disciple" (Luke 14:26-27). It is not going to be easy to live by Jesus' words.

I do not think I am better than anyone. I know my sin. I know my shame. I know the many millions of things I wish I could change about myself. I know that it is only by God's grace that I am His child. I sat this week in the darkness of depression. I had to make a hard choice, and the words that lashed out at me cut into my heart. I felt the words stab deep into the corners of my mind, and they became the image I projected on myself. *I am wrong; I am hated; and I am alone. How dare I? I should be ashamed. I should be condemned.* I could not find light; I could not find joy. I was swimming through the thoughts that tormented me while trying to cling to God's Word and find peace.

I have felt like Peter this week, denying Him at every turn. I know that God is my Provider; but as I talked about the good things in my life with an unbeliever, I allowed them to say I was lucky, even though I know that it is not luck that provides for my family of six on a one-income budget. It is not luck that keeps my old van running down the road with no problems. It is not luck that keeps my relationship with my husband good. I know that God has seen me through so many things, but I did not want to awkwardly insert God into our conversation. So instead, I just continued to let luck get the glory. That is not standing firm on my faith; that is letting my flesh rule.

I apologized for my stance, saying I could not go against my beliefs—like my faith in God needs an apology. I did not want to be shut out of someone's life. It hurts. But it would hurt worse to go against God. I hate that I am not bold and let fear win. I let fear make me apologize for my belief in God.

Tonight, I sat outside and watched the sun dip into the horizon. I told God that I would praise Him, anyway. I do not have all the answers, especially not the deep ones of this life that are hidden. I do know that whatever happens, I want to praise God. I want to stand in His presence having done my best at this thing called life—not because I want to be praised, not because I want people to think I am something special. I want to praise God because of Who He is and because He is special to me. He is my Source. When it is dark, there is no one else who can bring me back to the light.

I do not want to be the worthless salt that is thrown out into the darkness, as we read in Luke 14:34-35: "'Salt is good, but if it loses its saltiness, how can it be made salty again? It is fit neither for the soil nor for the manure pile; it is thrown out.'" Thank God for His forgiveness. Simon Peter was given forgiveness. He found grace, stood up in his faith, and grew bold. I want to live for God, to praise Him, and to speak His name in the presence of unbelievers. I want Him to be glorified and not "luck."

> *How lovely is your dwelling place, LORD Almighty! My soul yearns, even faints, for the courts of the LORD; my heart and my flesh cry out for the living God. Even the sparrow has found a home, and the swallow a nest for herself, where she may have her young—a place near your altar, LORD Almighty, my King, and my God. Blessed are those who dwell in your house; they are ever praising you.*
>
> *Blessed are those whose strength is in you, whose hearts are set on pilgrimage. As they pass through the Valley of Baka, they make it*

a place of springs; the autumn rains also cover it with pools. They go from strength to strength, till each appears before God in Zion.

Hear my prayer, LORD God Almighty; listen to me, God of Jacob. Look on our shield, O God; look with favor on your anointed one.

Better is one day in your courts than a thousand elsewhere; I would rather be a doorkeeper in the house of my God than dwell in the tents of the wicked. For the LORD God is a sun and shield; the LORD bestows favor and honor; no good thing does he withhold from those whose walk is blameless. LORD Almighty, blessed is the one who trusts in you (Psalm 84).

God is worth praising. He is worth losing everything in this life for—even family, even yourself. It is hard. I fail often; my flesh and sinful nature want to pull me away. I get caught up in the things of this world, but my heart's desire is to walk in His Word and trust in His unchanging grace. God's kingdom is like a treasure, hidden in a field. I want to go and sell everything I have for that treasure. How beautiful a thing it would be to stand as a doorkeeper in God's house.

Chapter 22

Starting Again

Therefore, if anyone is in Christ, the new creation has come.
The old has gone, the new is here!

2 Corinthians 5:17

Sunlight pours through my window. I want to soak in the warmth and breath. Spring feels as though it is close, but it is still months away. While resting in the window seat, my houseplants are soaking up the rays, too. I looked closely and noticed they were shooting off tiny, fresh, green leaves—new life. Outdoors, the trees are budding early, but that is Oklahoma for you. One day, it is snowing; the next feels like a summer day; give it a few days, and a tornado blows through. All the trees are getting excited about the early start, and tiny buds are appearing again. But if they are not careful, a winter frost might come through and damage the new growth.

It feels so good to stretch out and reach a new height, goal, or purpose. But the problem with growth is that it sometimes gets stunted. Sometimes, the growing pains are too uncomfortable. Sometimes, the workout hurts and leaves you sore. It is often easier to quit when it gets a little painful than to keep pushing. Although it is exciting to see a new start and a glimpse of where you are headed, obstacles and the winter freeze can slow you down. Pushing too hard and too fast into change can sometimes cause you to burn out quickly.

I have been on this journey of growth. Every time I feel like I am starting to sprout, there is another battle that slows me down, another storm that leaves me flattened. Today, I felt refreshed—like I could

131

conquer the world. Then I got kicked in the head by my cartwheeling, tumbling, whirlwind daughter. I did not feel like I could handle much with my aching head and was snappy. All I wanted was a nap. Instead, I ended up with five extra kids (my nieces and nephews), my mother-in-law, and sister-in-law all coming over for dinner and a play date. It was fun but exhausting, and I longed for that neglected nap. Things sometimes go differently than planned. Sometimes, we are cruising on the easy side of life; and then an accident, death, sickness, or kick to the head can send our lives reeling off course.

This is why we need to be mature Christians. Without a solid foundation of faith built on the rock of Jesus, we will instead become like sinking sand. We will crumble under the hard things of life and not be able to stand against the storms. I am an emotional Christian. I get highs and lows—days where I feel close to God, then a reality check hits, and I feel so distant from Him. We are a lot like plants. If we do not get watered, we start to dry out and die. Spiritually, we need Living Water. We need to be watering our minds with the Word of God. We need to be soaking up time with the Source of life. If we do not, we will wilt and be too weak to stand when opposition comes our way.

I took the kids on a field trip to see a basketball game with our homeschool group. I had planned it to be a fun day, but instead, my anxieties were high. Hormones and pre-monthly cycle emotions were raging. I just wanted to enjoy a game with the kids, but the day quickly went in the wrong direction.

Traffic to get there was crazy. I could not find parking. While I was stressed just trying the park the car, the kids kept asking hundreds of questions. Finally, after we found parking, my ten-year-old decided it was a good day to test me. He would *not* wear his coat, even though the threat of snow was hovering over our day. Granted, my patience level was already low because of the above-stated preexisting emotional/mental funk. I finally got him to put on a coat, draping it over his head instead of covering his arms.

Fast forward about three hours, my four-year old had spent the entire game climbing on me like a monkey, making sure I was talking to her instead of letting me watch the game. The kids wanted popcorn, a drink, and everything else; but I was trying to stay within our budget while still having fun. We did a little splurging but kept it to a minimum. Whew! I was tired, stressed, and strained, still trying to keep up with the Joneses and be a super fun mom. We left with another frustrating coat debate as we walked out into a cold rain. Why can kids not wear their coats? After a full day of trying my best to be a part of a group and yelling at my kids in the car between stops, I finally found an opportunity to leave after lunch, and I went home and cried.

God's there on the sunny days when life feels safe, easy, and fresh and on the cloudy, cold, bleak days when you are at your breaking point. What you do on the days in between—the everyday movement forward on your walk with God—matters. Even if you are strong in your walk with God, there are times when it is easy to crumble. When we crack, God is still faithful. That is when we pick up our pieces and start again.

Peter, the "rock" on which the church was built (Matt. 16:18), denied Jesus three times before the rooster crowed. He said he would never forsake his God, but when things got scary, he got scared. Then, after Peter saw Jesus rise from the dead, Peter still did not know what to do with himself. So, he gathered up his friends and went out fishing. Jesus had called him to fish for men, but Peter returned to the familiar in the middle of all the hard things. He went back to his comfort zone.

Jesus still made a point to redeem, restore, and remind him of his purpose. Jesus set him back on track. Peter got a fresh start—and even a yummy, home-cooked fish fry out of the deal. From there, he lived zealously for God, pouring his life into the ministry. He still had ups and downs throughout his life, but he relied on God to see him through.

God can give us a new start every day! I had a meltdown yesterday and forgot God's goodness, but He gently tugged me back to Him. God sent people to encourage and lift me. He reminded me that He would do abundantly above what I could "ask or imagine" (Eph. 3:20). He reminded me that He is my Provider. And the best part is that "because of the LORD'S great love we are not consumed, for his compassions never fail. They are new every morning; great is your faithfulness" (Lam. 3:22-23).

Sometimes, we get stuck in the muck of apathy and complacency and just need to refocus our lives. We need that fresh start. We need to purposefully and actively seek after Him. Matthew 5:6 Jesus says, "Blessed are those who hunger and thirst for righteousness, for they will be filled." We need to have that hunger and desire to seek after God. Sure, we will face opposition that will try and push us off course. The enemy might kick us in the head for our efforts. But we are promised in James 4:8 that if we "come near to God . . . he will come near to [us]."

A life dedicated to God does not have to be filled with Instagram-worthy moments. You do not need a warm cup of coffee steaming nearby while you write down Bible verses in your favorite leather-bound journal. It does not have to be a pretty day, early in the morning, with sunlight streaming through the windows. It does not require the smell of roses or honeysuckle to brighten your day. Sure, those things are nice, but our spiritual journey does not have to be picture-perfect. A thriving relationship with God involves repetition, consistency, and prioritizing Him, even if the day starts crazy. So, start again, my friend. Nourish yourself with the Word of God and grow with grace.

Bonica Brown

is a wife, mother, writer, artist, photographer, graphic designer, and children's pastor. She met her husband of thirteen years in college, where she graduated with an art degree from Northeastern State University in Tahlequah, Oklahoma. She and her husband are the associate pastors at their church, First Pentecostal Church of God in Fort Gibson, Oklahoma. They have been involved in youth and children's ministry at their church for over twelve years. Currently, she lives in Muskogee, Oklahoma, with her husband and four children, fourteen chickens, three dogs, two cats, a guinea pig, and several fish. She is a city girl who fell in love with the country life. Learning to grow a garden, make sourdough bread, can pickles, and homeschool her children have become the best parts of her life. Living in simplicity and thankfulness are her goals for the future.

You can find her at:
BonicaBrownBooks@gmail.com
www.bonicabooks.com

www.facebook.com/BonicaBooks

www.x.com/bonicabooks

www.instagram.com/bonicabooks

Ambassador International's mission is to magnify the Lord Jesus Christ and promote His Gospel through the written word.

We believe through the publication of Christian literature, Jesus Christ and His Word will be exalted, believers will be strengthened in their walk with Him, and the lost will be directed to Jesus Christ as the only way of salvation.

For more information about
AMBASSADOR INTERNATIONAL
please visit:

www.ambassador-international.com
@AmbassadorIntl
www.facebook.com/AmbassadorIntl

You make it possible for us to fulfill our mission, and we are grateful for your partnership.

To help further our mission, please consider leaving us a review on your social media, favorite retailer's website, Goodreads or Bookbub, or our website, and check out some of our other books on the following page!

Also Available from

Ambassador

International

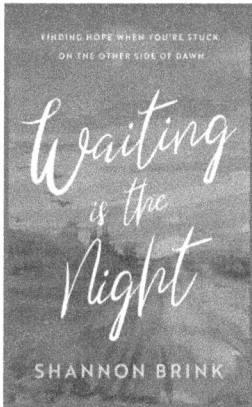

We all go through seasons of waiting, times when God just seems to have closed His ears to us and turned His back. During those seasons, it's easy to give up hope and lose heart. What can we learn from those times of waiting? Drawing from her own experiences and from the examples of God's people in the Bible who also experienced seasons of waiting, Shannon encourages the reader to hold on to the One Who created us. While waiting in the dark, cling to the Light.

When Kathy Vintson finds herself upside down with her underwear on full display at, she suddenly realizes just how chaotic the world can be, and she is reminded of the Crown Effect—that she is a daughter of the King, Whose unmerited favor is to love her, even when her granny panties are on full display. Using humor and humility as her guide, Kathy takes a deeper look into what it means to be truly loved by the King of kings and how to bask in His love and peace, even when the world feels like it is closing in.

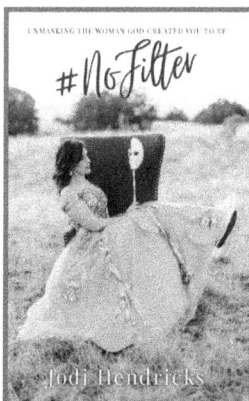

In #NoFilter: Unmasking the Woman God Created You to Be, Jodi Hendricks helps you challenge the filters that have enslaved you, discover the calling to which you've been called, and to bask in the truth that as creatures of the Creator Himself, you need no filter. The Almighty Who created you has had a plan and a purpose for you since you were knit together in your mother's womb, and He has called you to walk in a manner worthy of this calling.

www.ingramcontent.com/pod-product-compliance
Lightning Source LLC
Chambersburg PA
CBHW062112080426
42734CB00012B/2831